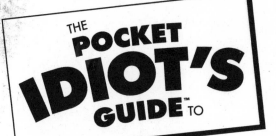

THE POCKET IDIOT'S GUIDE TO

Being the Mother of the Bride

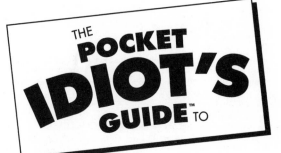

THE POCKET IDIOT'S GUIDE™ TO

Being the Mother of the Bride

Amy Zavatto

ALPHA

A member of Penguin Group (USA) Inc.

ALPHA BOOKS

Published by the Penguin Group

Penguin Group (USA) Inc., 375 Hudson Street, New York, New York 10014, USA

Penguin Group (Canada), 90 Eglinton Avenue East, Suite 700, Toronto, Ontario M4P 2Y3, Canada (a division of Pearson Penguin Canada Inc.)

Penguin Books Ltd., 80 Strand, London WC2R 0RL, England

Penguin Ireland, 25 St. Stephen's Green, Dublin 2, Ireland (a division of Penguin Books Ltd.)

Penguin Group (Australia), 250 Camberwell Road, Camberwell, Victoria 3124, Australia (a division of Pearson Australia Group Pty. Ltd.)

Penguin Books India Pvt. Ltd., 11 Community Centre, Panchsheel Park, New Delhi—110 017, India

Penguin Group (NZ), 67 Apollo Drive, Rosedale, North Shore, Auckland 1311, New Zealand (a division of Pearson New Zealand Ltd.)

Penguin Books (South Africa) (Pty.) Ltd., 24 Sturdee Avenue, Rosebank, Johannesburg 2196, South Africa

Penguin Books Ltd., Registered Offices: 80 Strand, London WC2R 0RL, England

Contents

Introduction

There's no doubt that being a mother of the bride is a joyous position. Seeing your daughter glowing with such happiness and anticipation of the new life she's about to embark upon with a man whom she considers her equal, her love, and her best friend— it's one of those moments in a parent's life when you say to yourself, "Well, now, I've done a pretty good job." It's a unique time of special bonding between a mother and daughter, when you both share your joys, your hopes, your past, and her future. It's truly a special time in your relationship.

It's also, however, a job you need to be well prepared to take on. It is not a position loaded with accolades or center stage for much, if any, of the festivities. In fact, even the bride's father gets more of a starring role during the ceremony and reception. But the mom o' the bride? What does *she* do?

Oh, you know, everything.

You are, for the entire planning process, right up to the wedding day, your daughter's right-hand woman (if you choose to accept this mission!). From counselor, to feather-smoother, to wedding planner extraordinaire, to financial consultant (and, in many cases, financial backer), to best friend, you've got quite a job in front of you. And that is precisely what we want to help you with.

How to Use This Book

From incorporating cultural traditions (and avoiding cultural clashes!) to helping your daughter pick out the perfect dress to throwing an engagement party to remember, this book is going to be a one-stop resource for all your questions and conundrums, and, hopefully, where you will turn to ease your frazzled nerves when needed. In between, you'll find useful bits of information in the form of sidebars scattered about to give you an extra charge of info, such as …

> **Wediquette**
>
> These boxes will give you helpful tips to keep things running smoothly during the planning process, all the way up to your daughter's big day.

> **Altared States**
>
> If you want to avoid the trips and traps during the planning process and the wedding, look here. Since weddings don't come with warning labels, we've provided you with a few to steer you clear of any pitfalls you might encounter.

Keepsakes

These just might be the most important bits of information you'll get. In this box, you'll find the real experiences of other mothers of the bride. They tell you in their own words what they did, how they got through it, and what a beautiful, positive experience it was in the end. Sort of like being a parent! Some moms wanted to remain anonymous, and for those we changed their names (just in case it's the same name as your cousin or sister or someone else you know—we don't want to start a family brawl over nothing!).

Acknowledgments

Thanks must go to all the beautiful, wonderful mothers who generously shared their stories and contributed their wisdom to this book: Theresa Perna, Ellen Steinbaum, Jane Ritzler, Helen Rahrer, Leila Tutela, Cindy Cho, and a few anonymous moms whose names may not appear, but who were just as integral to the wisdom bestowed as those who were named.

Big thanks also to Randy Ladenheim-Gil, a kick-ass mom and great editor, the remarkably patient and wise Mike Thomas, and the very astute Ross Patty and Megan Douglass.

Trademarks

All terms mentioned in this book that are known to be or are suspected of being trademarks or service marks have been appropriately capitalized. Alpha Books and Penguin Group (USA) Inc. cannot attest to the accuracy of this information. Use of a term in this book should not be regarded as affecting the validity of any trademark or service mark.

Mother of the Bride: The Job of a Lifetime

In This Chapter

- What being a mother of the bride is all about
- What is expected of you financially
- What is expected of you emotionally

Inarguably, there is no job more stressful, rewarding, and downright important as being a parent. From the moment your daughter came into your life, you have guided her, counseled her, cheered her on, taught her right from wrong, and loved her with every fiber of your being. You gave her all the things she needed to become the lovely, intelligent, capable woman she is today. And now she's getting married.

When you first heard the news, it probably filled you with a multi-level-parfait mix of emotions and reactions: joy, sadness, fear, pride, stress, love, nostalgia, dread, protectiveness. Any and all of the above, and maybe a few more to boot. Each of these reactions is completely normal, as being the mother of the bride means many things, emotionally and practically, such as:

- Your baby girl is undeniably all grown up.
- You are old enough to *be* the mother of the bride.
- You will inevitably be diving into your own memories of getting married, good or bad.
- You will learn a lot about both the similarities and differences you and your daughter have in taste, style, priorities, morals, music, food, marriage partners, tolerance levels, etc.
- You will be faced with the question of financing—partially, fully, or not at all—this soiree.
- You will be called upon to act as the unofficial hostess of the wedding, and possibly pre-wedding celebrations as well.
- You will more often than not have to act as an Ambassador of Goodwill between your daughter and a bevy of other people, and even between your daughter and yourself!
- You will find more strength, patience, and love than you knew you had.

And really, that's just the tippy top of the wedding cake.

This is the purpose of this first chapter—to let you know what is or might be expected of you so you can prepare yourself (in all the ways you'll need to be prepared) for the months ahead. We'll help you with the nitty-gritty of that preparation throughout this book, but first let's get you acclimated (or re-acclimated, as the case may be) with this big, crazy, stressful, wonderful rite of passage known as your daughter's wedding.

What Is Expected of You

Much has changed as far as what is and isn't expected from the parents of the bride. Some might say anything goes, and more often than not, that's true. No longer are parents locked into paying for the entire shebang, nor are the children necessarily expected to do everything the parents will them to do. Of course, weddings—as happy an occasion as they are—do tend to bring out strong opinions and emotions, and, with apologies to Charles Dickens, great expectations, too.

Being a mother of the bride is a lot like your regular ol' job of being a mom but with, frankly, a lot less up-front input. This isn't to say that your input is not needed, valued, required, or desired—quite the opposite. Your daughter is going to need all the help she can get. But whereas in your regular mom job, you rule the roost—making the rules and enforcing them as well—in your mom-of-the-bride job, using your skills of support, nurturing, and diplomacy will be a top priority.

Why? Because the most important thing to remember and to repeat to yourself over and over during the planning of this wedding, during the ceremony, and during reception is this: *This is not my wedding;*

this is the wedding of my daughter and future son-in-law. Unless your daughter doesn't want any part of the planning at all and leaves all the decisions to you (and some mothers and daughters prefer this arrangement), she will be calling the shots.

Keepsakes

"The thought that has gotten me through two sets of my children's wedding plans is, 'This wedding is *not about me* or what I want.'"

—Theresa, mother of bride Charlotte

With that in mind, this is a good time to prepare for what is, or could be, expected from you financially and emotionally. Of course, there are lists of responsibilities, and they vary depending upon who's writing them and what publication is printing them, in the same way that wedding rules (wearing black, wearing white, wearing red, and so on) vary depending on who's throwing the wedding. Following, though, are what we consider to be the updated semi-official traditional "list" of duties that fall under the domain of mother of the bride:

- With your spouse if you are married, consider and plan for what you will contribute financially.
- Help your daughter choose her dress and trousseau, as well as other wedding and honeymoon attire.

- Choose your own attire appropriate to the occasion.
- Make contact with the groom's parents.
- Make sure your attire and the groom's mother's attire are complementary.
- Help put together the guest list for the entire event and seating chart for the reception (this includes determining whom the groom's family would like to invite).
- Keep a tally of wedding responses.
- Make arrangements/reservations for out-of-town guests.
- If needed, help the maid/matron of honor organize a bridal shower; or, if she can't be the hostess, throw your daughter a shower yourself.
- Organize and host the engagement party.
- If needed, organize and host the rehearsal dinner.

Wediquette

Traditionally (and in all fairness to you) the shower and rehearsal dinner are not the responsibility of the bride's mother or the bride's parents in general. The shower is the responsibility of the maid/matron of honor, and the rehearsal dinner is the responsibility of the groom's parents.

- Act as the main contact for wedding professionals hired for the service and reception.
- Be your daughter's main source of strength, confidence, and comfort.

If that sounds like a lot to do, that's because it is. The good news is this is simply a list—a *guide*. What you choose to do and/or not do is something you are free to work out with your daughter and, possibly, your spouse. But do keep in mind the following when deciding what you will take on:

1. How much money you can contribute with ease (in other words, without making your day-to-day life uncomfortable or putting you in the poorhouse);

2. How much time you realistically have to devote to helping;

3. How much help your daughter actually wants or needs.

It's of the utmost importance that you consider and discuss all of this up front with your daughter. Neither of you will want to find out, in the middle of the planning process, that you've made an incorrect assumption about what the other wants, needs, or is able to do. Have a nice, calm, reasonable sitdown *before* all of the planning hullabaloo begins, and you'll be grateful later. Let's take a closer look at the financial and emotional expectations you may face.

Financial Responsibilities

Some brides' parents insist on paying for the whole shindig—ceremony to soup to nuts. In that realm, some feel it's their duty to plan everything for their daughter, while some prefer to foot the bill and let their daughter and future son-in-law (or, if you happen to live in progressive areas like Massachusetts or the city of San Francisco, daughter-in-law) plan it all themselves. Some parents pay for part of the wedding. Some pay for none. Regardless, the budget does play a starring role in the wedding plans. What follows is a list of financial responsibilities that, more or less, traditionally belong to the bride's kin.

Keepsakes

"I 'gave' the weddings, with discussion of all items with my daughters. I am one of those very opinionated and old-fashioned mothers of the bride who believes it's my party to give in honor of my daughter. They seemed fine with that, in fact maybe re-lieved not to have to attend to all the details. Our tastes are pretty similar and I can't think of any decisions we disagreed on."

—Ellen, mother of brides Judith, Meg, and Debra

- Engagement party
- Wedding dress and accoutrements
- Wedding programs

- Flowers (for ceremony and at reception if needed; however, groom's family is responsible for the bride's and bridal party's flowers, as well as the boutonnieres for the groom and groomsmen)

- Reception (place, food, entertainment, favors, etc.)

- Photographer and/or videographer

- Limousines or other forms of transportation to and from the ceremony and reception

- Lodging for bride's out-of-town family

Wediquette

Research hotels, motels, and inns near the site of the wedding and "block out" rooms for your guests. Many places will offer a room discount based on the guaranteed business, and will also provide you with a card with all the pertinent information, which you can send along with the official invitation. This saves you the time and effort of making individual arrangements for out-of-town guests and allows them to easily make lodging arrangements beforehand.

Again, it's of the utmost importance that you consider what responsibilities are financially viable for you to take on. If you and your daughter are clear on what items you can pay for from the get-go, it will make the rest of the planning go that much more smoothly.

Emotional Responsibilities

Your own experience getting married may well have created your opinions on how you would like to see your daughter's day unfold. Maybe your parents paid for it but insisted that the decisions, no matter how much you disagreed with them, be up to them. Maybe you got to call the shots, but your parents couldn't or wouldn't help you financially, leaving you with a daunting number of decisions and a shoestring to make them on.

Keepsakes

"I believe we act in a particular way as a reaction to our past experiences. Questions [about being a mother of the bride] conjured up memories of forty-two years ago, when my opinions of planning weddings were formed. I decided then that if I ever had children who wanted to get married, their weddings would be *their* weddings."

—Theresa, mother of bride Charlotte

Altared States

You won't be able to help reflecting on your own wedding experiences, and this might be a lovely time to share them with your daughter. But if your own experience falls mostly to the negative, avoid dwelling on the sadness of that memory if you can. It's not that you can't or shouldn't ever share this with your daughter, but don't allow those bitter memories to become part of your daughter's day. When your daughter wears "something blue," you don't want it to be the past.

Whatever your own experiences, as the bride's mother you should be fully prepared to:

- Take great care in how you phrase your words with your daughter. Remember how emotional and stressful it is to be the bride? It might be on the tip of your tongue to say, for instance, "Oh, no, that dress looks terrible on you!" when your daughter twirls out of a fitting room in something that you feel is less than gorgeous. Instead, flip on that Internal Editor switch and say something like, "I'm not sure about the that one. Let's try a few different cuts to see what's the most flattering for you and get back to it."

- Be a mediator. Sometimes, the pressure and emotions of planning a wedding (and, most importantly, joining her life to another person's) can make it difficult for a bride to keep her wits about her. You know your daughter well enough to sense when she's at the end of her rope with wedding vendors, wedding attendants, family members, her future husband, and so on. Be ready to counsel your daughter or, when appropriate, step in and deal with a situation that could benefit from a neutral third party. If all goes well, you may be able to apply for a job at the United Nations when this is all over!

- Reassure siblings. If the bride has siblings, they may well get "Sixteen Candle" syndrome. (Remember poor Molly Ringwald when her parents forgot her birthday in lieu of her sister's wedding?) This is an adjustment for them, too, so do your best to remember to give them some extra attention or, better yet, include them in some of the planning process. That way, they won't feel left out and it turns some of the preparation into a full-on family project (not to mention gives you the opportunity to delegate!).

- Pay some extra attention to your future son-in-law. Grooms often (sometimes by choice, sometimes by circumstance) can be left in the dust during the wedding preparations. Try to include your future son-in-law in the pre-wedding hoopla. Shoot him an e-mail to ask his opinion or invite him on a wedding errand. It's also a good way to get to know him better (if you don't feel you do) and to make him feel part of the family.

- Remember dad. If you and the bride's father are together, remember that he's going through the same cauldron of happy and sad emotions that you are, and maybe some you're not. Although it's more common than not for young women to have left the nest long before they choose a partner in life, and fathers don't "give" their daughters away, it still can be a gut-wrencher for a dad to see his baby girl perform a rite of passage that may not feel so long ago for him. Talk to each other about how you feel and remember to give each other a pat on the back for raising such a lovely, independent, intelligent young woman.

- Have a strong shoulder at the ready to lean or cry on.

- Remind your beautiful, wonderful daughter how proud you are of the woman she's grown into and that, really, it's all going be just fine.

Chapter 2

Ready to Wear: Helping Your Daughter Select a Dress and Finding Your Own

In This Chapter

- Shopping for a new dress
- Wearing your dress/family dress
- Picking your dress
- Coordinating with the mother of the groom

There are a million and one wedding details that you and your daughter will pore over. But the one that will likely take up more energy and time than selecting the menu and place (and possibly even the groom!) is that all-important show-stopper, the wedding dress. To help your daughter choose the perfect dress for her special day, you're going to have to be part fashion maven, part psychologist, part diplomat, and part soothsayer. And then, of course, you have to pick out your own outfit (and try to select one that won't clash with the mother of the groom's). Never fear—in this chapter, we'll get all those seams straight, buttons buttoned, and hemlines just so.

The Search for the Perfect Dress

Helping to pick out the wedding dress is a great opportunity for some memorable moments between a mother and daughter. The instant she steps out of the fitting room in that perfect-for-her dress will be one that you'll both remember the rest of your days. Of course, you should be forewarned that it can also be a part of the wedding planning that's susceptible to stress, high emotions, and potentially hurt feelings for both of you (maybe you're starting to remember this from your own wedding planning!). Why? Because this is an area where many potential conflicts come into play, like:

- Differences in taste—what you consider stunning, your daughter might not want to be caught dead in and vice versa.

- Expectations—maybe you're hoping your daughter will want to wear your wedding dress (see "Wearing Your Dress or Family Dress" later in this chapter for more on that topic).

- Financial concerns—the price of a wedding dress can run anywhere from $100 to $10,000! And that's not counting the accoutrements or alterations.

There are also issues of self-image that a bride goes through and needs reassurance for—issues of weight, of beauty, of making the right decision. When you spend a day (or several) trying on dress after dress, after a while it's pretty easy to get lost in a haze of tulle, chiffon, and matte satin. She's going to need lots of reassurance from the most important mentor in her life: you!

Keepsakes

"If Deb or Christina picked out a dress and then had second thoughts and I really didn't care for it, I would encourage them to look at more dresses. I would say to go with their 'gut' instinct. You know when it is the right dress; you just know when you have it on. If I did not like the dress and they did I would say so and why. If they really loved the dress and I did not care for it, I would suggest trying on a few more dresses. Or I would suggest trying on a veil, jewelry, and other accessories to convince me that this was *the* dress."

—Jane, mother of brides Debra and Christina

The first thing you need to do before you even hit the road on your shopping mission is arm your daughter with the most important dress-searching secret there is: a strong, solid ego. Tell her how beautiful she looks that day. Don't allow her to become victim to bad body image syndrome or feelings of insecurity—let her know that you think she's never looked more lovely. Feeling confident and good about herself is the best dress-shopping tool your daughter can have, and you're just the person to boost her ego when she needs it most.

Second, sharpen those skills of diplomacy. In the end, your daughter has to be the one who loves the dress and feels comfortable and beautiful in it—not you. While your opinion is likely to be the most important one she will seek, you will need to separate your feelings of what *you* would want to wear and what looks best on your daughter. This might be tricky at times for a few reasons:

1. Your vision of the wedding might not be the same as hers. Maybe you prefer a traditional look, but your daughter likes more modern dress styles, or vice versa. Your daughter also might have a more casual affair in mind, but you're picturing a formal affair. Sit down with a bridal magazine or two before hitting the pavement and get a feel for what she prefers. You'll have a better idea of what she has in mind (not just for the dress, but for the wedding in general) and can set your sights on helping her seek out the best option in this style.

2. She might ask a few trusted girlfriends along for the shopping trip who are guiding her toward what they would want to wear as opposed to what looks best for her. Again, in this situation, diplomacy is key. Suggest

trying on other dresses in a positive manner, as suggested previously. Also, ask your daughter's friends to help you search for some more dresses (if there is no dress attendant helping you). When you are alone with them, tell them what style you think flatters your daughter's figure best and ask for their opinions. That way, you are gently guiding them but also keeping them in the process, as well as finding out why they prefer certain styles to others.

3. She might prefer a style that doesn't flatter her figure. If this is the case, try to guide her to styles that are more suited to her body type. Be honest with her; just be gentle with your honesty. In other words, don't say, "Ugh! That looks awful on you, sweetheart!" Instead, use those great skills of diplomacy you've honed over all these years of parenting and say, "You know, dear, that's a lovely dress, but I'm not sure it's exactly right for your body type. For the heck of it, let's try on a few more styles just to see—that's why we're here!" Be truthful, but be positive.

On the latter note, there are a few tricks of the trade to help your daughter accentuate her best physical attributes, and play down the ones she's not as fond of:

- For a small bust, avoid high necks. Accentuate neck, shoulders, and clavicle area. Scoop necks, "boat" necks, sleeveless dresses, and spaghetti straps are all good options. If your daughter is small-busted and petite as well, avoid large details like puffy sleeves. Although many wedding-dress styles these days are veering away from that, puffy sleeves make a small woman look like a child playing dress up. She'll be lost in all that material. Empire waist dresses are good to try here as well. They add the illusion of more up top, in addition to the illusion of height.

- To add more curviness to a straight figure, try full skirts and a V or sweetheart neckline. However, straight figures can also look fantastic in long, straight dresses—just make sure the shape of the dress emphasizes rather than de-emphasizes the waistline.

- To de-emphasize a large bust, try a high, straight neckline or jewel neck and simple sleeves. Also, the simpler the better on details.

- For a bottom-heavy figure, avoid full skirts. An A-line dress style can be very flattering in this case (although A-line tends to flatter just about any body type).

When your daughter does find "the" dress of her dreams, ask the shop owner or manager a few important questions: a) Ask how long it will take for the dress to come in once ordered; b) Make sure they order the exact color your daughter tried on; c) Find out approximately how many fittings will need to be done; d) Get an estimate on how much alterations will cost, and ask for it in writing. Also, if you and your daughter both like a dress but are unsure and want to keep looking around, write down the brand, style number, and price. If it's off-the-rack and there's only one left in your daughter's approximate size, ask the shopkeeper if she'll hold the dress for 24 to 48 hours for you. She may require a small deposit for this accommodation.

Finally, when you and your daughter head out on this all-important wedding mission, have a strategy. You'll get a lot more accomplished in a much saner way if you have a clear agenda set out for the day. Make sure you:

- Map out your stops ahead of time. You don't want to spend the day aimlessly driving or wandering around. Write down three or four spots, the address, phone number, and basic directions ahead of time.

- Allot no more than three to four hours per dress-hunting trip. Any more than that and you'll both be exhausted, cranky, and unable to make a clear decision.

- Find out if you need an appointment. While many bridal shops encourage walk-in customers, there are others that require you to make an appointment. Call ahead and make sure so you don't waste time and gas driving to a store for nothing.

- Know what you can/want to spend ahead of time, what your daughter is contributing if anything, and find out if the stores you both wish to visit can accommodate that price range. How? Call them! Ask what the average price of a dress is in that shop and tell them what you can afford to spend.

● Eat something! That goes for both of you.
  There's no need to gorge on a hungry-man
  special at your local diner, but eat breakfast
  and stop for lunch. A hungry bride and
  mother can make for some cranky shopping.

Keepsakes

"If my daughter chooses a gown that I
don't like, I'll ask her friends to give her
their opinions. If they tell her it's hideous,
she'll forgive them much sooner than she
would me. If they all agree with her that
it's lovely, then maybe I'm out of sync, will
re-evaluate my opinion, smile, and let it be.
It's her wedding. Actually, I'm prejudiced;
my daughter always looks lovely to me."
—Theresa, mother of bride Charlotte

Wearing Your Dress/Family Dress

Your daughter has asked if she can wear your dress
or the family heirloom wedding dress that's been
handed down from your great-grandmother for her
wedding, and you're utterly touched by the gesture.

The first thing to do is assess what shape your wedding gown is in. If it appears to be in good condi-
tion, great! *Do not*, however, go straight to the dry
cleaner. The dress may appear to be okay, but you
should first have it assessed by a dressmaker or tailor.

There could be loose seams, small tears, etc., that should be repaired *before* handing it over to be cleaned and doing more (and possibly irreparable) damage to the dress.

Also, it's entirely likely that at the very least some alterations will need to be made (assuming you aren't changing it) and the dressmaker will be able to tell if this is or isn't possible before you shell out a couple hundred dollars to get it cleaned. The dressmaker will let you know whether or not the dress should be cleaned before alterations begin.

Keepsakes

"I remember the 'picking out the dress' part with each of [my daughters] as so wonderful and so much a part of the whole experience. With the first wedding, my daughter saw a dress she liked, didn't want to even try it on until her sisters and I were there, and, when we were, bought that without ever looking at another. My second daughter described a dress she had seen in a magazine and I realized it sounded like my wedding dress! So we had mine remodeled a little for her. With the third daughter, who was married after my husband died, my daughters and I spent a day together and she tried on a few dresses and when she got to 'the one' we all knew it."

—Ellen, mother of brides Judith, Meg, and Debra

What if your daughter wants to make some major alterations to the dress? For instance, the style might be too out of date, unflattering to her figure, or just not exactly her taste. First, make sure you're okay with this—if you're not, be honest. Bad feelings don't make for a positive mother-of-the-bride experience, for you or your daughter. More than likely, we're betting you'll be tickled pink that your daughter wants to wear your dress, and will probably agree that alterations need to be made. Consider …

- Keeping the bodice and, if your dress was a full skirt, adding on a straight skirt, or vice versa.
- Keeping the skirt and adding a new bodice.
- Adding, removing, or altering sleeves (e.g., if the sleeves on the original dress were elbow length, changing them to capped sleeves).
- Adding or taking away details (bows, flowers, tulle, beading, etc.).
- Changing the neckline.

Keep in mind that making alterations to the original dress may be for more than just style purposes (although that's certainly a factor at times); it's also, and most importantly, to flatter your daughter's figure. Although some of us come out as the spitting image of our parents, some of us don't! If you and your daughter decide that major alterations are necessary, have them made to suit her body type.

Wediquette

A borrowed veil does more than just fulfill the old adage and save some money—it also is believed to bring good luck.

Selecting Your Dress

There are a few rules to follow when selecting your own attire for your daughter's wedding. Of course, the most important thing (just like helping to pick out your daughter's dress) is that you feel good in the dress/outfit. It should be comfortable and flattering first and foremost. You should also ask your daughter if there is a color or style she would prefer.

Next, you need to know what kind of affair this is going to be before selecting your attire. For a formal affair, a full-length or cocktail-length dress is appropriate to the occasion. For a semiformal wedding, tea length is appropriate, or you might want to go the Diane Keaton route and wear a flattering suit. If the wedding is to be informal, a casual dress or suit is fine.

The next thing to consider is color. The ones to avoid are fairly obvious: black, white (of course!), anything too loud or bright. You don't want to draw attention away from the woman of the hour—your daughter! All eyes really should be on her. That doesn't mean show up in a robin's egg blue potato sack, but when choosing the color (and style) of your outfit, think classic and demure and complementary to your own coloring. Never, ever try to outshine the bride.

There are a few other important factors to consider when selecting your outfit. One is to complement the dress color of the bridesmaids. You don't necessarily want to wear the same color that they will (in fact, you should probably avoid it), but you shouldn't clash with them, either.

Keepsakes

"I asked my daughter what color she had chosen for the bridesmaids, and I assume I'll look for something that coordinates with that color, unless she tells me there's a specific color she wants me to wear. I think it's wrong for the mother of the bride or groom to use their dress as a device for attention; a sort of competition. I would attempt to be an object of pride, style, and decorum for my children. Having someone remark that my dress was stunning in comparison to everyone else's would be ridiculous to me."

—Theresa, mother of bride Charlotte

The second factor is coordinating the color and style of your dress with your daughter's future mother-in-law. It is tradition that the mother of the bride selects her dress first. However, the groom's mother might not be aware of this rule of wedding etiquette. It will be up to you to contact her and let her know the general style and color of the outfit you plan to wear so she can coordinate appropriately. Your daughter may even want to give her future mother-in-law some color/style guidelines as to what she would prefer in order to complement the bridesmaids and the mother of the bride. If you are comfortable and get along well with the mother of the groom, ask her to join forces with you and shop together. That way, you'll be sure to have complementary colors and styles.

Finally, make sure that you allow enough time for alterations. Just like with your daughter's wedding dress, you may need one or several fittings before the big day. Make sure you give yourself at least a few months' lead time so you won't be down to the wire.

Chapter 3

Making a Budget and Saving Money

In This Chapter

- Who pays for what?
- Traditional responsibilities versus what you can afford
- Money-saving tips
- Keeping your ducks in a row (deposits, contracts, and following up)

We could debate all day whether money makes the world go 'round, but it undeniably plays a large role in a wedding. Of course, when we think about marriage and what a milestone it is in your and your daughter's lives, it's not the first thing you think about. But it *is* a necessary part of making this event happen, and the sooner you and your daughter figure out who's responsible for what, the easier the process will go.

If your daughter and her fiancé are paying for the whole shebang themselves, you can skip this chapter. If you are doling out any cash at all, though, stay right here. We're going to help you plan out your expenses, save you a little green with helpful wedding-planning suggestions, and make sure you get exactly what you paid for.

What Must Be Paid For

We touched on this briefly in Chapter 1, so you have an idea of what expenses are involved. Before you read any further, though, do one crucial thing: Sit down with your daughter and her fiancé and discuss what you can contribute and how this will be done. For instance:

- You are financially able to pay for the entire wedding and will deal with the various vendors on your own with input from your daughter on what her preferences are.

- You are financially able to pay for the entire wedding, but your daughter would prefer to deal with the actual nitty-gritty of the planning, all the way down to dealing with the vendors. In this case, you can release checks to her as needed or provide her with a lump sum in the beginning so she can dole it out as necessary.

- You are paying for part of the wedding and your daughter and her fiancé are financing the rest. In this case, you can give her the

lump sum you've decided you can contribute in the beginning, or she can ask that
you handle certain set costs of the wedding,
like the flowers, photographer, or transportation.

- You are paying for one or two important
items, like the wedding dress and/or accoutrements. In all likelihood you will be present when the dress is being selected and can
pay for it, alterations, and so on, at the dress
shop. Or, if you can't be present, you can
provide your daughter with the money for
the item beforehand.

Wediquette

Ask your daughter to give serious thought
to which items of the wedding are of the
most importance to her. If she doesn't care
that much about engraved invitations, but
her dream is to arrive at her wedding in a
Rolls, or a simple dress is more her style but
the food has to be top notch, then you can
shift some money according to her priorities. Prioritizing is key!

In each of these scenarios, one very important
thing needs to happen: You must look at your
finances and decide what, *exactly*, you can afford.
Once you decide on a number, then that sets you
and your daughter off on the right track. For

instance, if you know that you can spend a maximum of $500 on the flowers, you're not going to spend your and your daughter's time chatting with the florist who did the flowers for Jennifer Aniston's wedding. If you know you can provide up to $1,000 for a wedding dress, you won't be spending the afternoon at Vera Wang (unless, of course, your daughter decides this is what she wants and is able to kick in the extra costs).

The cost of the average wedding with a guest list of around 150 to 175 people in the U.S. runs around $20,000, give or take. In their "State of the Union" report in 2000, *Bride's* magazine took this one step further and broke the average overall cost down by region and came up with the following:

- Northeast: $32,000
- Southeast: $17,000
- Midwest: $19,500
- West Coast: $18,000

Where does all this money go? *Bride's* further breaks down these numbers into average amounts in 18 categories:

1. Invitations, announcements, thank-you notes, other stationery: $775
2. Flowers: $1,253
3. Photography and videography: $1,253
4. Favors: $240
5. Music (ceremony/reception): $745

6. Ceremony (officiant, site): $248
7. Transportation (limousine, etc.): $427
8. Attendants' gifts: $299
9. Wedding rings: $1,060
10. Engagement ring: $2,982
11. Rehearsal dinner: $762
12. Wedding dress: $790
13. Headpiece/veil: $150
14. Attendants' apparel: $720
15. Mother-of-the-bride dress: $198
16. Groom's attire (rental): $100
17. Ushers' attire (rental): $400
18. Reception (average of 186 guests): $7,246

Keepsakes

"My daughter drew up a spreadsheet detailing all the expenses. We discussed the individual costs [and] compromised when needed. Initially we released checks to her, as the individual vendors needed to be paid. Closer to the actual day, we gave her the estimated remaining balance knowing if there were unexpected costs that we would cover it. For example, my husband extended the open bar for the entire evening. If there were little things she wanted to add, she picked up those costs."

—Leila, mother of bride Liz

Once you decide how much you can afford, you should look at the individual costs traditionally paid for by the bride's parents and what these items might entail. Remember, these are just guidelines—you can decide to pay for the groom's tux, the honeymoon, the flower girl's dress, or dancing bears, if that's what you feel is important. The so-called traditional financial responsibilities should be used as guidelines to clarify what's involved in a wedding's expenses—not commandments. It's up to you and your daughter to decide which ones are going to fall under your or her (or her future in-laws—they may very well want to share the expenses) responsibility. Following are some things to consider with each of the general areas of expense—and, most importantly, suggestions for how to save money!

Engagement Party

If you choose to host a party for your daughter, you'll need to decide whether you plan to do this in your home, cook yourself, cater in-house, hire some local assistance, or rent out a restaurant for the occasion. While it may seem like doing it yourself is an automatic money saver, it can still run you quite a bit of cash. The best way to save money on a party in your home is to be organized. Why? If you aren't, and you order too much food or buy too many decorations or rent too much china or make any of a number of other common mistakes, you'll end up wasting money you really can't afford to throw out the window right now. See Chapter 5 for how to throw great (and reasonable!) pre-wedding shindigs.

Keepsakes

"My daughter and her fiancé are financing their wedding. I offered to take care of certain expenses, but they declined our offer and wanted to be able to take care of the wedding on their own. [However] the most important thing was to buy my daughter's wedding gown, one that would make her feel the most beautiful."

—Susan, mother of bride Cindy

Wedding Dress and Accoutrements

Wedding dresses can range in price from free (yours or a friend's—but don't forget about the alteration costs) to $10,000 if you're looking at couture. However, an average, middle-of-the-road price for an off-the-rack traditional gown is between $500 and $1,000. For a "designer" dress, you can expect to pay between $2,000 and $5,000.

There are several ways to save money on a dress. If your daughter is of medium build (a 6, 8, or 10), try sample sales. Most large local papers have a wedding supplement twice a year (usually, around the winter holidays and in the spring), which would list advertisements for such sales. The back of bride magazines are a good spot to hunt, as well. The best place to look, however, is the Internet (see Appendix B for a list of great sites to check out right now, or go to your preferred search engine and type in "discount wedding dresses" and your state, or check out www.weddingzone.com, which will tell you what's available in your state). You can also help her look for a dress on consignment, for sale in the classified ads of your local paper, or on an auction website like eBay.

Altared States

While some people might tell you the more simple the gown, the cheaper it will be, this isn't always necessarily true. Don't mistake "simple" for unadorned. While beadwork is one of the obvious details that you'd think could raise the price of a dress, it's the fabric and layers of it that can raise the price. Also, dress styles today lean much more toward the simple and elegant than the ornate, and this does not necessarily translate into less money. The name of the designer also plays a large role in the cost of the dress.

Also (and this is something that you should keep in mind for just about everything you'll spend money on), if something is labeled as "bridal," it's not unusual for the price to elevate. If your daughter is thinking about a less traditional wedding, look for dresses that aren't necessarily for a bride—bridesmaid, formal wear, even (don't laugh) "prom" dresses. If this is a consideration for your daughter, you might end up spending no more than $200 on a dress. Once you've found a dress, make sure you shop around for alteration prices as well. The shop you buy the dress in might be charging more than is necessary and you can find a better deal at another shop, at your local tailor or seamstress, or if there is a dressmaker in your area, he or she might do alterations as well.

Announcements, Invitations, and Wedding Programs

There are lots of ways to save money with printing costs for a wedding. Prices can go up or down depending on the kind of paper used, accoutrements (ribbons, blotter paper, cord), and printing (raised lettering, embossments, regular laser jet printer, do-it-yourself printing at home on your own personal printer). But even with traditional invitations with raised lettering, you can still save money.

First off, make sure you have your guest list finalized so that you don't order too many invitations or programs. Next, blotter paper (that see-through sheet of onion paper that you find in some formal wedding invitations) is an item that you can easily cut out. Back in the day when the ink on an invitation actually needed to dry, the blotter paper served to keep the lettering from smudging or getting all over the inside of the envelope. Obviously, it's not a necessary extra today and can save you a bit of money if you forgo it.

Also, many formal invitations come with three envelopes—the one that is addressed to the recipient, the one that holds the actual invitation, and then the response card envelope. Consider ditching the invitation-holding envelope (again, this is another leftover relic from those ink-drying days). You can also make the response note a postcard rather than a note that needs yet another separate envelope (just make sure that the price of those envelopes isn't less than the price of a postcard stamp—then you're wasting rather than saving money). You can also opt for regular laser printing instead of formal, raised lettering as a cost-cutting measure.

Wediquette

Think about the people you, your daughter, and her fiancé know who might be able to lend a talent to the wedding. A talented musician for the ceremony or reception, someone with a good eye and hand for making bouquets, a friend who's got a flair for calligraphy, a judge or clergyperson, or just that one great creative type who has an unending supply of original, great ideas. Somewhere in your kin and kind, there are folks who can lend a talent and help you cut your budget. Not only that, but a close friend or relative adding something to the ceremony or reception makes the occasion more personal and special.

Lighter-weight paper stock will save on postage for you, as will standard-size invitations (as opposed to oversized ones, which can cost more). If the wedding is informal, you are really on a tight budget, and you don't mind veering far off the traditional bridal path, consider asking guests to call or e-mail responses.

But one of the biggest money-saving tips for invitations? Make sure all names and addresses appear and are spelled correctly. Money spent buying replacement envelopes for misprinted ones is money thrown out the window.

Flowers

Depending on the time of year your daughter and her fiancé choose to wed, the size of the bridal party, whether or not there will be flowers at the ceremony, and how she plans to use them at the reception, flowers for the ceremony and reception can range anywhere from a few hundred to a few thousand dollars. How can you keep to the low end of that spectrum?

For one, if your daughter is getting married in a church, temple, or synagogue, find out first and foremost if flowers are allowed for ceremonies. It would be an awful waste of money for your florist to show up with baskets of flowers for the altar only to be turned away. Second, if the wedding coincides with a particular holiday, there might already be flowers there, and thus the decoration issue is solved.

At the reception, think simple. Cascading lilies and roses exploding from pedestal vases on all the tables is going to cost more than a demure mix of in-season flowers in a low vase. (It also makes conversation easier around the table!) Ask your local, trusted florist what's in season for your daughter's date and go with that. Or you could eliminate the table flowers all together and instead make the centerpieces potted plants such as African violets or primroses. They can also double as the favors if you group one for each guest or couple in the center of the table. Also, candles are cheap and make for fantastic mood lighting. Fill a shallow, broad vase with water and dot with floating tea lights. If you want more of a floral showing at the table, try making napkin rings from artificial flowers and florist wire.

Reception

This will be, by and large, the biggest expense of the wedding, and usually costs a minimum of $10,000. Spending can really add up here. First and foremost, start early and shop around. The longer you and your daughter wait to scout locations, the fewer options you will have, in locations *and* price point. Second, ask your daughter to consider having the wedding on Friday night or Sunday afternoon, as Saturday night will always cost you top dollar. Consider an "off-season" wedding, too. Having the wedding in late fall or early winter as opposed to spring will save on money. Next, try to secure a venue that already has the basics: chairs, tables, linens, silverware, china, glasses. If they don't, you'll have to rent them, and that adds up to more money out of pocket.

With food, make sure you're clear about your budget with the caterer and that they allow you to taste the food beforehand. It won't matter that you saved a bundle if the food is awful. Also, the more choices you offer your guests, the more expensive it will be. Keep the hors d'oeuvres to a minimum and limit the dinner option to no more than two, unless you can safely avoid an option at all. If there are vegetarian guests or guests with dietary restrictions, you can easily and—more than likely—inexpensively accommodate those few people while still keeping costs down. As with flowers, you can save money on the menu by going in-season and skipping the exotic and the imported.

Liquor is an area where many people worry that, if they limit the bar choices or open-bar hours, guests will get cranky. For one, this is a wedding, not a tailgate party. Second, it's nice to have fun and enjoy spirits at a celebration, but you want to make sure your guests get home in one piece. Limiting the bar hours (in other words, closing the bar an hour or two before the reception is over) will cut your costs and give you peace of mind.

Consider serving one special, festive cocktail during the cocktail hour, champagne for the toast, and then beer, wine, and soft drinks during dinner and dancing. This will save you a chunk of change on beverages. You also might ask if the reception spot will allow you to supply the liquor yourself and purchase spirits at a discount liquor shop, wine merchant (most wine shops discount vino by the case by 5 or 10 percent), or beer distributor. Watch for sales advertised in the papers and ask for a bulk discount.

With entertainment, if your daughter and her fiancé don't have their hearts set on live music, opt for a DJ. If they do, though, you might be able to scout out local universities (or even high schools) for budding musicians looking to make some cash and get more performing experience. This isn't to say hire the local garage band, but check with the music departments to see if there are any clubs or groups specializing in classical (for the ceremony) or jazz (the cocktail hour), or big-band, rockabilly, Fifties, or other easily danceable music for the reception. If you have a CD burner, a good ear for music, and the time, put together a few mixed CDs of your daughter and future son-in-law's favorite songs, as well as some good universally pleasing dance music. This also makes a nice keepsake for the couple after the wedding.

Altared States

Thinking about having the wedding in your backyard to save money? Think again. Backyard weddings can cost as much or more than those at a restaurant or reception hall because each and every item that is already present in the latter has to be rented for your backyard: shelter (a tent); generator; lighting; heating (if it's even remotely chilly); silverware; china; linens; tables; chairs; toilets; and so on. Add it all up and your simple backyard wedding will be a big backyard budget buster.

Photographer and/or Videographer

One of the best ways to save money on photos and video is using your resources. Is there someone in your family who's always got the video camera out to film every occasion? Ask that person to videotape the ceremony and part of the reception if he or she doesn't mind (likely, the person will be happy to do it). For photos, put disposable cameras on each table at the reception (with directions; many people are unclear how to operate them) so your daughter will get lots of candid shots of the reception, and also ask family or friends who are amateur photographers to snap some formal and informal shots. You can also check with your local university or high school for budding photo and video pros looking to get some experience under their belts. As with professionals, though, make sure you are very clear about the shots you wish taken and ask that they don't experiment with technique (we know a bride whose amateur photographer decided to shoot the whole wedding using a technique he had just learned, and all but a few pictures were ruined).

If getting a professional is of extreme importance to you and your daughter, ask for recommendations from friends or family members who have had a recent wedding. Make sure you view the vendor's work beforehand and are very clear what you want done, how much you will be charged for film and developing, video and copies, and if the proofs are free (they often are). Make sure the vendor isn't going to add extras (special effects and so on) that will cost extra and appear dated soon after.

Transportation

Limousines or other forms of transportation to and from the ceremony and reception are a good place to cut corners if you need to. First and foremost, the only way to really save is to compare. Contact several limousine services in your area and find out what they charge so you have an idea of the range. Try both the Yellow Pages and the National Limousine Service (see Appendix B) for names of vendors in your area.

Once you do, find out what's included in that price. Are they offering a stocked bar or champagne? If so, ask to eliminate that. Think about it this way—when you go to a restaurant, there's always a mark-up on liquor and wine. It's going to be the same in a limo. If you want, buy a bottle of champagne yourself. You can get a great bottle for twenty or thirty dollars, which will inevitably be a lot cheaper than the limo price.

Consider foregoing the white limo (or SUV limo or Humvee limo) for black or silver, as some companies charge more for the former (remember: once something is dubbed "wedding," the price usually goes up). You can also get in touch with an antique car club in your area to inquire about rentals or rent a luxury vehicle from a regular car rental agency. If the bridal party is very large, consider asking them to provide their own transportation to and from the wedding and reception.

Lodging

For your close out-of-town relatives, the best way to save money is, of course, to put them up in your own home if you have the room. However, most hotels offer bulk rates for weddings, so if you plan to reserve a block of rooms for others as well as your own relatives, you'll be able to save on your family's lodging.

Keepsakes

"I have two daughters and made four weddings (two each). They were informed at the second wedding that any future weddings (God forbid!) would be at their own expense."

—Celia, mother of brides Emily and Ann

Get It in Writing: How to Make Sure You Get What You Pay For

Whatever you pay for at your daughter's wedding, you must insist on getting the terms of your agreement with the vendor in writing. If you don't, you're making yourself vulnerable to unlimited costs and expenses above and beyond what you agreed to pay for, as well as the possibility of having a miscommunication and not getting what you asked for at all.

Each basic contract should contain:

- The name, address, and contact information of the vendor
- The date the contract was signed by both parties (you and the vendor), as well as the date and time the service(s) are to be provided
- Your name, address, and contact information
- The exact name and location where the service(s) is to be provided, as well as contact information for that location
- An exact, detailed description of what service(s) are to be provided
- The amount of time the service(s) will be provided, whether any breaks will occur during the service(s), and how many
- The total cost of the service(s), as well as the amounts of the deposit(s) and final payments and when they are to be paid
- If there are staff members, what they will be expected to wear
- If you are expected to feed the vendor and staff
- The total number of staff (waiters, band members, photography assistants, etc.)
- Any additional charges the vendor can charge (taxes and gratuities, insurance, travel fees, hourly charges if the service goes over the allotted time, assistants, cancellation charge, equipment, special effects, extra copies, extra videos, etc.)

Altared States

Beware of vendors who say they'll knock the tax off or discount the service/ product if you pay cash. You will have no receipt and, thus, no recourse if something goes wrong. Try to pay for items with your credit card so you have an automatic receipt, and if you are paying cash, make sure you get a receipt from the vendor.

For the reception, make sure the contract also states:

- Which room(s) the reception will be in
- The approximate number of guests attending
- The exact cost per guest
- Whether or not you require announcements or an emcee
- When the place will be accessible to you if you are decorating or need vendors to enter for set-up purposes
- The exact menu specifications (hors d'oeuvres, dinner, dessert) and whether this is a sit-down meal or buffet
- The exact drink specifications (what beverages will be served, whether it will be an open bar and how long)
- Any special meal requirements for your guests and how much that costs, if different from the other guest price

For the photographer and/or videographer, make sure the contract also states:

- If not the vendor you speak with, the name of the photographer/videographer who will be providing the service(s)
- The total number or photos and/or videos
- The total number of proofs and whether or not they cost extra
- How much extra photos and videos, above and beyond the number promised in the basic contract, will cost
- If there are any special effects, techniques, and so on, that will be used in photos/videos
- The packaging the product will come in (album style, page style, video case, etc.)
- The date when the photos/videos will be ready

The bridal industry, while certainly packed with lots of nice people who love weddings and want to help you and your daughter plan a splendid affair, is still a business. Favor purveyors, halls, photographers, and wedding dress shops are there to make money, and price accordingly. While there are certainly many fair-shake vendors around, you should beware of items that cost more than they should simply because they have become part of the blinding white-out of tulle, satin, chiffon, and lace—and make sure you get anything you buy in writing. It protects your finances and, most importantly, your daughter's wedding day.

Chapter 4

Making the Guest List

In This Chapter

- Who invites whom and who gets invited?
- Making multiple-tiered lists
- What to do about kids, single guests, and far out-of-towners
- Who sits where?

An entire chapter devoted to the guest list? Absolutely. It may seem like a no-brainer—call upon your near and dear to attend the wedding of your lovely daughter and her soon-to-be husband. The guest list, though, is the biggest determination of how much the wedding is going to cost (which, in all likelihood, if you're reading this book, is something you're concerned about). As we saw in Chapter 3, there are lots of factors that can influence the cost of a wedding, but the guest list is by far the biggest.

Also, making the guest list can start to seem a bit like walking in quicksand: You didn't notice any danger at first, but then ... plop. You're slowly sinking and have no idea how to get out. In other words, you and your daughter are fighting; suddenly you think her soon-to-be in-laws are the most ungrateful and ungracious creatures on the planet, your Aunt Agnes isn't speaking to you, and your future son-in-law keeps bringing up the word "elope."

Oh, yes. And where will you seat all these folks?

In this chapter, we'll help you get your list together, avoid busted bank accounts and hurt feelings, and figure out where to seat all your potential celebrants as well. Got a pen or a PC? Then let's go!

Making the List and Checking It Thrice (or More!)

Let's start out with the biggest, most important point to remember in this chapter: Even if you're paying for the whole wedding, this is your daughter's day. Filling the room with people she and her betrothed barely know or have never met, and *none* of her near and dear, is going to make the day memorable, just not in the happy way she would have preferred. It's fine to invite people who are important to you, your husband, and your family, but not at the expense of your daughter's own important guests (many of which will overlap with your own, if you think about it).

According to tradition, the guest list is split between the bride and her family and the groom and his family. Of course, if you're paying for the entire wedding, you might feel within your rights to add more to your own side. This is fine unless at, say, a wedding with 200 guests, you have 180 and the groom's family has 20. Again, this is your daughter's wedding day, not an occasion to keep up with the Joneses or use it as an opportunity to get "payback" for all the weddings you've been to and bought presents for. Certainly not at the expense of your daughter's happiness. That is too dear a price to pay.

Keepsakes

"To make her life easier, I supported the decision-making process and only challenged her when it was really important to us. For example, she and her fiancé only wanted people they knew to be invited. My husband comes from a large family of first cousins of whom we have been invited to most of their children's weddings. It would be an insult in our heritage to not include them. He also was a partner in a company for which he wanted to include the other partners. (The bride did know these folks since she worked there as a teenager and as a young adult.) Since my husband also wanted his golf friends, I negotiated to include my cousins and friends that I've known for over 20–48 years. Thus her guest list of 150 swelled to 235. Examples of supporting her decisions: She chose the reception hall, band, photographer, basic menu, etc., with only a few suggestions from us."

—Leila, mother of bride Liz

However, that is not to say that you cannot and should not share this day with people who are important to you and your family. Here's how to get started.

Size

At this point, you've already allotted how much you can spend or contribute to the wedding and hopefully your daughter has decided what kind of wedding she wants. This is, of course, the key to how many people can share in the day with her. Your daughter may want a large celebration or a small, intimate wedding. Everyone has their own idea about the size of a guest list—what seems like a large wedding to you might seem medium to your daughter. There's nothing scientific in this, but here's a basic guideline to give you an idea:

- Small—under 50 guests
- Medium—between 50 and 125
- Large—over 125
- Am I at the right wedding?—anything over 250

Wediquette

Consider sending out "save the date" cards four to six months before the wedding, especially if you know many people will be traveling from far away and need to make travel and hotel arrangements for the wedding.

Wediquette

When making the guest list, be sure the names are spelled and appear exactly as they will on the invitation and that you have their proper mailing address, phone number, e-mail if applicable, their relationship to the bride or groom, and whether or not they will be attending. One mother-of-the-bride we know kept two boxes—one that said "yes" and one that said "no" near where she put the mail and simply tossed the response cards in the appropriate box as they came in, then sorted through them and noted the responses on her official guest list. After the wedding, it's handy to keep the list around when gifts are being opened so that the bride and groom can note what was given for appropriate thank-yous.

Depending on the restaurant, inn, banquet hall, caterer, or what have you, you will now be able to price out reception areas to see if they fit your budget. The guest list is an area where lots of compromises will inevitably need to be made, and when you start looking at reception spots, you and your daughter will be faced with some potential areas where you must rob from Peter to pay Paul. If it's important to your daughter that she has a very elegant, formal wedding and your funds are not unlimited (and whose are?!), then the $150 a head price is going to dictate who gets moved from the B list to the C list. Harsh as that may sound, you will be forced to make cuts to the guest list based on finances. However, if faced with guest cuts, your daughter might be willing to go less formal in order to accommodate her desired celebrants. The priorities of the day will become very clear.

Tiers

Now, speaking of B and C lists, here's a trick that can help you to make allowances where there was no room on the initial list. It might seem a bit mercenary, but we prefer to look at it as just plain practical.

When you and your daughter sit down to make the final list, divide the guests into tiers of lists of A, B, C, and, if needed, D. Your A list should consist of those close family members (grandparents, sisters, brothers, aunts, uncles, and so on) who take precedence. In other words, the people you can't imagine having a wedding without. Also on this list should be the officiant and his or her spouse (yes, this is protocol) and the parents (if they're not already invited) of the flower girl(s) and ring bearer. In addition, keep in mind that anyone who was invited to the engagement party or shower must be on the A list (so plan these gatherings accordingly!). It is in extremely poor taste to invite people to the pre-wedding celebrations, accept their gifts, and then leave them out of the main festivities.

Your B list should consist of first cousins, closest friends (of your daughter, her fiancé, you, and the future in-laws), nieces, and nephews. The C list should have friends, important and/or close work associates, teachers, neighbors, and second cousins. The D list is reserved for newer or social friends and distant relatives.

Keepsakes

"I felt that it was necessary for the bride's family to invite the in-laws to dinner. And discuss with them the wedding plans and the number of guests that each family could or would invite."

—Celia, mother of Emily and Ann

Once you have these lists firmly down on paper (or on disc), send out invitations to the A list guests and those on the B list that fit into your allotted numbers. General protocol is to send the invitations six to eight weeks prior to the wedding, but we advise that you lean more toward sending them eight to twelve weeks prior. This allows you more time to receive yes and no responses and, therefore, to send out invitations to those further down on the lists when you know you have room for them. As long as the invitees have four weeks' notice, you are perfectly within the appropriate time frame for inviting them.

Altared States

> Whatever you do, don't discuss the tier system you've created or the exact date you plan to send invitations with anyone other than your husband, daughter, her fiancé, and possibly his parents. It's a common practice, but not everyone understands the financial practicalities and, when they learn that they are on any list other than A, will have their feelings hurt.

Children, Dates, and Other Conundrums

Children can be a sticky point at a wedding. Some people feel they are a vital, important part of the celebration, and others don't think they belong at a formal or semi-formal affair. This is for you and your daughter to decide—there are no right answers. Once you do figure out whether or not children will be permitted at the celebration, you can simply let people know by writing the names of the parents and the children on the invitation, or just the names of the parents (in other words, the children are not invited).

It is never, ever appropriate to specify on or in the invitation that children are not welcome. As the mother of the bride, you may be called upon to use those finely honed skills of diplomacy here and speak to certain family members, friends, and so on, who are not clear on whether their children are allowed. There are a couple of rule-bending, crowd-pleasing things you can do to accommodate your guests, however:

1. If you have room in your budget, hire a baby-sitter (or two or more, depending on how many children there are) to watch children during the ceremony and reception for those people who cannot make other arrangements.

2. Specify an age limit. In other words, children 10 years and older may come, but you would prefer that younger ones not attend (this is where a hired sitter for the celebration comes in handy, also).

Also, if the bride and groom have children of their own from prior relationships, then you should allow children to attend, period. It will probably be more entertaining for the kids anyway if there are people their own size to socialize with as opposed to a room full of grown-ups!

Another issue that gives brides and their moms pause is dates of guests. Must each single guest bring a date, or is it okay to invite only the guest on his or her own? That depends. If the nonmarried guest has a boyfriend or girlfriend or lives with his or her significant other, then, yes, that invitee should absolutely be invited with a guest. However, if the invitee is not seeing anyone, then it isn't necessary to invite that person with a guest. It's nice to do if you have room in the budget, but if you don't, it's perfectly acceptable to ask that person to attend on his or her own. How do you specify this on the invitation? The same as with children above—write the name of the invitee on the invitation and the name of the guest, if you have it, or just "and guest."

Altared States

If a guest phones you or your daughter and asks to bring a guest, although he or she was not invited with one, you should not feel guilty about telling that person no (unless, of course, he or she is informing you of a significant other you were not aware of). It's difficult not to give in to pressure, but if one person brings a date, then everyone should be able to bring a date. Stick to your plan and no (or fewer) feelings will be hurt.

What about people you'd like to invite who live far away? Should you assume that they won't be able to travel the distance and not invite them? Or invite them anyway because you're worried about hurting someone's feelings? The best thing to do with guests who live far enough away where they'll have to hop a plane is to call and feel them out, or ask directly if you're comfortable enough. If they say yes or that they aren't sure, absolutely send an invitation. If it sounds like they can't make it, send a wedding announcement or a card instead.

Duck, Duck, Goose—How to Seat Your Guests

The RSVPs are in; you know who's attending your daughter's big day (well, minus the inevitables who neglect to tell you they're bringing a date at all). Now where do you put them?

Unless your daughter plans to have a very casual let-them-sit-where-they-may type of wedding, you're going to have to assign tables to your guests. First, you will need to know what kind of table set-up is being offered by the reception site. Are the tables round? Square? Rectangular? And, most importantly, how many people will they seat *comfortably*? Without this knowledge, you can't create a seating chart, so make sure you have this information before beginning to assign who goes where.

 Altared States

When you visit potential reception sites, make sure you take note of the table sizes and how many chairs comfortably fit around them. If the reception hall is a little too eager for your business, the manager might try to convince you that squeezing a few extra folks around the table is perfectly fine. It's not. If you're clanking elbows and unable to pull your chair out, there are too many seats. Don't let anyone talk you into an uncomfortable situation for your guests.

Set aside some time and sit down with your daughter, her fiancé, the final list, a pad of paper, and a pen (or your laptop if that's easier for you), and do the following:

- Create categories for guests; bride's family, bride's friends, groom's family, groom's friends, your friends, groom's parents' friends, and so on.

- Label the categories A, B, C, etc. For instance, bride's family is A, groom's family is B, and so on.

- Put the category letter next to each guest's name on the list.

- On your pad of paper or on your PC, write or type the headings Table 1, Table 2, and so on.

- Under each heading, use your A, B, and C categories to divide guests appropriately among the tables.

Voilà. You've created your seating chart. Now we're making this sound very, very easy—and, really, it is. But the reason it's vital that you do create this chart with your daughter and her fiancé on hand is to make sure that people are seated in appropriate groupings. For instance, let's say your daughter's fiancé has two friends, a man and a woman, who used to date pretty seriously and had an ugly break-up. You probably don't want to sit them at the same table, right? Right. But it's unlikely you'll know the nuances of these relationships, just as you wouldn't necessarily expect your future son-in-law to know that Aunt Rose and Aunt Susan have a long-standing rivalry and tend to get into rather loud fights when they get within a few feet of each other. Knowing relationships is key when seating people at tables.

You should also try to make sure you divide table groupings in even amounts. It's a bit awkward to have four tables of eight, six tables of four, and three tables of ten. Make sure you have a balanced number at each table. Why? For one, the room will look awkward with varied amounts of people at the tables. Unbalanced tables can on occasion cause chaos— the four bored people sitting at table 10 look long- ingly at all the fun the eight people are having at table 6, and decide they're going to take matters into their own hands and sit where the action is (we've seen it happen!). Bingo—instant chaos.

Further, think about the practicalities of where you are seating people. Is table 5 next to the DJ's speak- ers or the band? Don't put your elderly relatives there as they're not likely to appreciate the boom- boom-boom of your daughter's favorite hip-hop get-up-and-dance song from college or your son- in-law's love of the Ramones.

Finally, it is appropriate to seat immediate family closest to the bride and groom's table as it is gener- ally considered a place of honor.

Chapter 5

Part(y) and Parcel: Engagement Parties

In This Chapter

- Why you should throw an engagement party
- Who to and how to
- Types of parties
- Some professional catering tips

After your daughter and the love of her life made their announcement of betrothal, immediately you began to think about plans for the Big Day. Before that occasion, though, there is a small but important celebration that you may want to host: the engagement party.

Typically, the engagement party occurs soon after the engagement is announced and is arranged and hosted by the bride's parents (the rehearsal dinner is traditionally the responsibility of the groom's folks). There are a couple of very good reasons to throw an engagement party for your daughter and future son-in-law. First, it's a lovely way to honor the happy couple and celebrate their upcoming nuptials. Second, and maybe even more important, it's an opportunity to bring the families together and break the ice.

In this chapter, we'll help you figure out how to plan and where to have a pre-wedding celebration to remember.

Who to Invite

Who to invite to the engagement party is, of course, a matter of whom you, your daughter, and her fiancé would like to celebrate with, as well as how much you can afford to spend and how much room you have to comfortably entertain people.

Wediquette

Usually, the announcement of an engagement is made by the parents of the bride. Most newspapers have a standard form for you to fill out, which you can either pick up at the paper's office if it's close by, call and have sent, or, in many instances, access online. They will likely have a pre-set time that it appears (several months before the wedding, a few weeks before the wedding, etc.). Just check with your daughter and her fiancé to make sure all the information is exactly as they'd prefer it to appear (the correct title of schools, degrees, spelling of groom's parents' names, and so on).

The only absolute, bare-bones, must-haves on the list are immediate family members—parents, grandparents, and siblings of the bride and groom. Aunts, uncles, and cousins are generally considered extended family, but, of course, if your family is close-knit and it would be unthinkable to leave them out, then they should be on your bare-bones list as well.

If the bride and groom know whom they plan to ask to be in the wedding party, then those individuals should also be invited. It is not necessary to invite them with a date; however, if they are married, engaged, or living with a significant other, it is in good form to invite that person's partner, as he or she will be a wedding guest as well.

Beyond this, close friends of the bride and groom or of the respective families should be invited if there is enough money in the budget and room in your home to comfortably host them. We recommend that business associates, more distant relatives, and acquaintances be left off the guest list for an engagement party, as adding them will swell the number of guests and make it difficult to find a reasonable cutoff point. (You know how that goes: "If I invite so-and-so, then I have to invite so-and-so because she'd be insulted!") Keep it as close, intimate, and simple as you can.

Altared States

> Never, and we mean never, invite someone to the engagement party (or bridal shower if you are hosting that as well) who isn't invited to the wedding. Although you might have the best of intentions (for instance, you know the wedding will be very small and you want to try to include people on the pre-celebration since you won't be able to accommodate them at the main event), you will only end up hurting feelings and insulting friends and family. Another no-no: Don't include registry information in the invitation to the engagement party. While it's become more common for people to give gifts at this occasion, it is not traditional and therefore not expected.

Party Planning 101

Pending budget and time restraints, the sky's the limit with the type of party to throw for an engagement. For our purposes here, though, we recommend keeping the engagement party to family and close friends. While large engagement parties are not unheard of, it's easy for them to turn into something that more closely resembles a wedding than a gathering to toast the bride- and groom-to-be. You don't want your guests to leave the engagement party thinking, "So what's the wedding going to be like?!"

First, unless your last name is Trump, the reality is you're going to have budget restraints, and blowing a lot of cash on an engagement party is unnecessary and should not be expected. Second, as we mentioned above, one of the prime motivations for having an engagement party is to allow the families to break the ice and get to know each other a little. If there are 200 people milling about a catering hall, there won't be much opportunity for intimate conversation. If there are 20 wandering around your living room and dining room, your chances of getting to know each other are much better.

If you don't have the room or simply don't want to host the party in your home, it's fine to have the party in a restaurant. However, much of the reception-planning advice in this book applies here, albeit on a smaller scale (get everything in writing, plan ahead, and so on), so in this chapter we focus on hosting an engagement party at home since that will require more of your personal time, talent, and elbow grease.

Speaking of, whether it's a sit-down dinner, cocktail affair, or easy afternoon brunch, there are some basic planning guidelines that will make your job easier:

- Give yourself at least two months' lead-time for planning.

- As this is a special party with a very particular guest list, you want to have a date that accommodates all or as many guests as possible. We recommend choosing three or four possible date options and, via phone or email, finding out which is the most amenable to family and/or friends, and then getting the invitations out to set that date in stone ASAP.

Wediquette

Can't host the party yourself? It's perfectly okay to check in with a close family member or friend whose home is better set up to accommodate a gathering. Make sure that you have a firm idea of the number of guests so there aren't any surprises. An appropriate follow-up gesture? Hire a cleaning service to get their home spic and span after the party!

- Consider choosing a theme or, if possible, having the party coincide with a particular holiday. This allows you to more easily pick your menu and decorations.

- On that note, party-up the atmosphere with three simple tips: 1) Adjust the lighting. If your everyday light bulbs are bright, consider a lower wattage and/or softer-toned bulbs to create a mood more conducive to a gathering (as opposed to reading!). 2) Remove clutter. Clutter can take many forms, from the obvious (your piles of unread papers and magazines and unsorted mail) to the overlooked (a piece of furniture that takes up space but doesn't offer seating, a place to put food, and so on.). Survey your home for removable items and store them away for the festivities. 3) Don't wait until the last minute to think about the music. Pick out several CDs that provide good background music for the occasion and have them lined up and ready to go.

Wediquette

A great time-saving organizational tip? Take your platters, serving bowls, and so on out of their storage spots and stick a Post-it on them with the dishes you plan to make. This might seem ever-so-slightly over the top, but it helps you to assess what you have, what you need, and how the presentation of food will appear.

- Don't go overboard on the menu, the amount of food you plan to order or make, or the level of difficulty involved in preparing it.

- If you are cooking, try to have as many things as possible that can be prepared at least a day ahead of time. Of course, certain dishes will have to be made the day of, but the more you can do ahead of time, the more time you'll have to relax and enjoy your daughter's celebration yourself.

Wediquette

Decorations aren't necessarily party streamers or silly cutouts. This is a serious step in your daughter's life, so consider leaning more toward simple and elegant rather than a kid's party. (We know—it's still hard to think of her as an adult!) Consider using in-season flowers around your home, candles, and linens in a color that's in step with the season, holiday, or theme. If it's a particular holiday, you may well have the bonus of your home being already decked out, so, voilà! There are your decorations.

- Find out if your guests have any food allergies or if there are any vegetarians in the crowd. You don't want to go to the trouble of preparing a shrimp etouffee if half the crowd is allergic to shellfish and the other half eats only plants.

- Assess your inventory. Based on the menu, do you need or have enough platters? Serving utensils? Dishes? Eating utensils? Chairs? Room at your table if it's a sit-down dinner? Coasters? Glasses? Coffee cups? A coffee urn? Sternos? Chafing dishes? Toothpicks? Think about each thing you plan to serve and how it will be presented and consumed.

- Ice! Even if you have an ice-maker in your fridge, don't overestimate the amount it can churn out. Make sure you have some extra bags on hand the day of the party. A good rule of thumb: Estimate about two pounds of ice per guest.

- Assess your skills. If you have never made dinner for more than four people, this probably isn't the time to experiment on serving 12 guests at a sit-down. Do what you are confident you can do. And for the things you can't, get help. Round up volunteers from your family and friends; hire your or your daughter's favorite local gourmet store, deli, or restaurant to make platters or dishes.

- If you plan to have your home professionally cleaned before the party, secure the service at least a month ahead of time. You don't want to wait 'til the week before only to learn that they're all booked up.

The best way to ensure that your daughter's engagement party (or any party, for that matter) will be a success is to plan ahead. Leaving too much (or, in our opinion, anything!) to do at the last minute risks not just the success of the party, but your own ability to enjoy yourself during the festivities (yes, you are supposed to do that). Plan ahead to ensure a party that goes off without a hitch.

Pick a Party

Of course, now you need to decide what *kind* of party you'd like to have. Will it be casual? A little more formal? A small group? More than 20 people? Then consider one of the following.

Altared States

No matter what kind of party you have, if there's alcohol served, make sure your guests are sober before they get behind the wheel of a car to drive home. If they aren't, do your best to persuade them to stay a little longer. This is a happy occasion and you want to make sure it stays that way.

Cocktail Party

Consider a cocktail party if you will have more than 12 guests. A cocktail party is a great way to get people mingling. The simple act of providing choices of food and drink at different stations around a room immediately gets even the shyest person circulating.

A cocktail party is a good gathering to have if you're trying to break the ice between family and friends before your daughter's wedding day. It's a good party to host for someone whose cooking skills lean more toward novice than confident cook, and also enables you to serve a wider variety of foods, so it's easier to satisfy many tastes.

Instead of having a stocked bar, which can be expensive and difficult to maintain during the party, offer one festive "theme" cocktail or punch, along with an easily paired red and white wine, like a merlot, pinot noir, dry Riesling, or Prosecco. And, of course, make sure you have plenty of soft drinks on hand as well. Estimate two to three cocktails per guest, and three to four soft drinks.

Try to think of your food in the same way, too. Use hors d'oeuvres that can easily go with a white or red. Consider versatile crowd-pleasing cheeses like manchego; dried sausage on crusty Italian or French bread; mushrooms stuffed with bread crumbs, fresh sage, and parmesan cheese; bite-sized nibbles of sliced beef; and a sprinkling of mild blue cheese baked in puffed pastry.

Try a pinot noir from Oregon or Sonoma or a crisp semi-sweet Riesling with the following recipe for East/West Salmon roll-ups. These are easily prepared the night before the party, and all you need to do is slice them just before guests arrive:

Salmon Roll-Ups

16 oz. cream cheese, softened

¼ cup sour cream

½ cup sun-dried tomatoes (in olive oil)

1 tsp. grated lemon peel

4 dashes Tobasco

6 10-inch flour tortillas (if you prefer to use a fla-
vored tortilla, that's fine)

2 bunches washed arugula

salt

1 medium red onion, minced

12 oz. smoked salmon

In a medium bowl, combine cream cheese, sun-
dried tomatoes, sour cream, lemon peel, Tobasco,
and cilantro until smooth (a food processor works
best if you have one).

On a flat surface, take a tortilla and lightly moisten
it on one side. Spread the sun-dried tomato mix-
ture in a ¼-inch-thick layer over the tortilla, stop-
ping at about ½ inch from the edge of the tortilla
all around.

Cover the lower third with a layer of the salmon,
the middle third with a sprinkling of red onion,
and top onion with a layer of arugula. Roll from
salmon side up to form a cylinder shape. Wrap in
wax paper.

Repeat with each tortilla until all six are prepared.
Refrigerate overnight or morning of the party. Just
before the party is slated to begin, take roll-ups out
of fridge and slice each tube into one-inch bite-
sized pieces. Serve.

Altared States

Avoid spices and flavors that are over-powering and linger on breath or fingers after touching and eating (i.e., garlic, raw onion, pungent cheeses, and so on). Bad breath isn't the best tool for getting to know new people!

Dinner Party

If you will have 12 guests or fewer, consider a dinner party. A seated dinner party requires that you put a bit more thought and effort into the gathering, but for a more intimate number, they're worth the effort.

For a seated dinner in your home, we recommend that you do not have more than 12 guests. Unless you're used to juggling the duty of hostess and cook like a pro, the stress involved with a sit-down for more than 12 people is too much to handle.

Barring any dietary restrictions, a roast is an impressive and easy way to feed a large number without a lot of running around. Avoid anything where the individual portions must be sautéed separately. Don't double up on side dishes—offer one starch and one vegetable, and salad to start or finish with. If you are serving wine, one standard 750 ml bottle will pour about five glasses.

Altared States

> Be sure to find out if any of your guests have dietary restrictions or allergies before planning your menu. There's nothing worse than putting a lot of effort and/or money into a meal only to find out that your guest of honor is a vegetarian and you're serving rack of lamb. It's embarrassing and deflating to you and the guest. Of course, you might assume that someone with dietary restrictions would let you know beforehand, but often they don't!

Brunch Gathering

A brunch gathering can be tailored to any number of guests. Like the cocktail party, it's a great gathering for a cook who is less sure of her skills. A brunch can be impressive *and* inexpensive at the same time—a very nice combination!

If you decide to organize a brunch to celebrate your daughter's engagement and gather those near and dear, we recommend going buffet-style, using chafing dishes for items that need to be warm. Some suggestions for the menu? Try a frittata or quiche. For those who like eggs in the morning, these baked dishes are easy to make and easy to keep warm. Plus they hold up well (much better than a tray of scrambled eggs!). If you want to serve breakfast meat, opt for sausage instead of bacon. Sausage holds up better than bacon in a chafing dish, as the latter tends to get soggy. A fruit salad and/or green salad are always a welcome treat, and make sure to have a nice bread-and-spread tray, too. Tip: Bagels are best because they don't necessarily need to be toasted. Provide cream cheese, butter, and jams alongside.

Caterer's Tips

We checked in with expert caterers Kyle and Tom Ritzler, both Culinary Institute of America-trained chefs who run a successful catering business in the Hamptons and own The Common Ground Café, a tapas bar/bakery/café in Shelter Island, New York. Here's what they had to say about creating a successful affair:

- Hors d'oeuvres: "I like to have a minimum of at least six hors d'oeuvres passed with a minimum of four to six pieces per person."

- What's popular: "Shrimp cocktail, mini crab cakes, filet mignon crostini, skewers, spring rolls."

- What to avoid: "Stay away from chicken satay or anything with peanuts or peanut sauce—lots of people are allergic to peanuts."

- Main dishes: "With the way people are eating nowadays, you need to allow 4 to 6 ounces of protein per person. People aren't eating like they used to eat!"

- Side dishes: "Usually we allow 4 ounces per person. Most people generally are not going to eat more than half a cup of green beans."

- Cake size: "For 20 people, a 10 inch round cake should do it, although be careful how you slice it [in other words, don't serve pieces that are too large—they probably won't finish them and there won't be enough to go around]. For a sheet cake, a 9 × 12 will feed 20 people."

- Things to prepare the day before: Cake, pastas ("For things like lasagna, it's better to cook them, cool them, refrigerate overnight, and reheat—it always tastes better."), blanching of vegetables, washing of lettuce.

- Things *not* to prepare the day before: Do not cook meat the day before because it will dry out. Also, do not cut up fruit the day before because it doesn't hold up well. However, do make sure you purchase fruit a few days ahead of time so that it's ripe for the party.

- What not to put on the menu: "Make sure you're not putting something on the menu that's available in August, like beefsteak tomatoes, and the party's in October when there aren't any fresh beefsteaks around!"

Finally, Kyle and Tom recommend that if you're cooking the food yourself, have a mini-dinner or hors d'oeuvres tasting a week before so you know how long it will take to cook the items and can adjust any seasonings or other ingredients that aren't to your liking.

One more tip: If possible in the space you have, try not to position all the food (specifically, the hors d'oeuvres) and drink in one spot. You want to try to ensure that people have a reason to circulate. You want to create a natural flow throughout the rooms designated for the party, as well as make sure there are plenty of tables to set down plates and drinks (and don't forget the coasters!).

Whichever type of party you decide to host, remember that the point is to gather, greet, and meet. And celebrate, of course. The more organized you are when planning the party, the more successful you will be in achieving this goal.

Chapter 6

In-Laws for Life

In This Chapter

- Why you should extend yourself to your daughter's future in-laws
- Ways to get acquainted
- Avoiding culture clashes between the families
- How to be a good mother-in-law

Mention the words "mother-in-law" or even "in-law" in some circles and the jokes start flying. They seem at times positions more in line with the Wicked Witch of the West or her evil monkey henchmen than valued family members. Does it have to be this way?

Oh heavens, no. While it's true that there are mothers-in-law out there with agendas that have little to do with trying to do what's best for their daughters and sons-in-law, and in-laws in general who seem to always say black when you say white, most of us really are just trying to do the right thing—we just don't always go about it the right way (or at times aren't necessarily dealing with reasonable counterparts). In this chapter, we're going to help you to navigate the sometimes rocky road of in-law relations with your rep intact—and your family, too!

Meet the Family

Meeting anyone for the first time can be a little awkward. And when it comes to your daughter's future in-laws, multiply that times a hundred. These are the people who produced the love of your daughter's life, after all (and vice versa for them!), so of course you're both going to be scrutinizing each other a bit (well, maybe more than a bit).

Keepsakes

"You don't treat them as in-laws. You treat them like your friends or relatives. Treat them with respect."

—Cindy, mother of bride Susan

That's all fine and to be expected, so it's best to meet and greet *before* the wedding. While there are no "official" rules as to who should extend themselves to whom, as the mother-of-the-bride you should take the initiative. Waiting for the rehearsal dinner for this first awkward meeting probably isn't the best idea. We know one bride whose families didn't meet until just this occasion—and it was a disaster. The bride's family was very American in customs and the groom's was very old-world Italian, which made for many a misunderstanding during the evening. By the time the night was over, the bride's father felt insulted by the groom's father, the mother of the groom was a nervous wreck, and the bride and groom? Well, they just felt terribly disappointed at how poorly the evening before their wedding had gone.

The good news is you can avert disaster simply by arranging a friendly meeting beforehand. You can do this in a few ways. If you know you have a common interest like golf or tennis, you can invite them for an afternoon on the green or court. Probably more customary is an invitation to join you for dinner at a restaurant that's midway between where you each live, or you can invite them over to your home for a brunch, lunch, dinner, or backyard barbecue, depending on how formal or informal you wish to be.

Altared States

Meeting the future in-laws is not an opportunity to show off. While it's perfectly fine to pull out your best dishes and stemware, don't brag or try to be showy. The point of this meeting is to establish a friendly rapport, not impress them with your acquisitions (that goes for them, too!).

Should the "kids" join you? Well, that all depends on what makes you feel most comfortable. If your daughter and her fiancé would like to join, then absolutely include them. They might serve as a good ice-breaker, as they're the reason you're getting together in the first place. If you are comfortable with and would prefer to meet the parents without the kids around, that's perfectly fine. Your daughter and her fiancé actually might be more nervous about the meeting than you are!

As for navigating the evening smoothly, try to steer conversation toward topics that are safe and not generally thought of as potential landmines (in other words, politics, religion, money). Stick to topics that are of mutual, amicable interest. The wedding, of course, is a safe bet, but avoid getting too into detail if you know there are some kinks that your daughter and her fiancé are working out with his folks (issues about the ceremony, the guest list, the location, and so on; ask your daughter ahead of time!). Tell them about you and your husband if you're still married, and ask about them. Talk about the kids; tell them some great things about your daughter they might not know and ask questions about their son (this is actually a great opportunity to learn some of his likes and dislikes, what he was like growing up, where he was raised, and so on).

Keepsakes

"It is important to get to know your daughter's future in-laws so you can have some deeper knowledge of her husband-to-be. It is good to know his background, his growing-up years, where he has been, and where he is going. What drives him!"
—Jane, mother of brides Debra and Christina

If an intimate dinner feels like a little too much pressure to you and/or your husband and you plan to throw an engagement party for the happy young couple (see Chapter 5 for tips on throwing a fantastic pre-wedding affair), then that is also a good social occasion to meet and greet. Just make sure that you actually *do* spend time with them at the party and make them feel comfortable and welcome.

If your daughter's future in-laws live farther than driving distance, that might make meeting face-to-face beforehand a little tricky if not impossible. Still, there are a few ways to get acquainted, the most obvious and easy being to pick up the phone and call them. Introduce yourself, say how excited you are about the upcoming wedding, and how much you're looking forward to making their acquaintance. You can also write a letter, or if your future son-in-law's folks have e-mail, shoot them a quick e-note. If they aren't very chatty, that's okay. Your mission here is not to force a close relationship, but to pave the way for the relationship you will have with each other from now on. Extending a welcoming olive branch sets a good tone for future meetings.

Keepsakes

"To get acquainted we gave an engagement dinner party in our home and invited the bridal party and their spouses, the bride's close relatives, and the groom's close relatives. Everyone knew the purpose was to get acquainted and be friendly. Anyone who didn't want to do that, didn't come!"

—Theresa, mother of bride Charlotte and groom Tom

The most important reason for all of this is that these are people whom your daughter will likely, hopefully, know for a very, very long time. You may discover that her fiancé's parents have a lot in common with you and you may make some wonderful new friends; you may get along fine but never see each other outside of special occasions for the rest of your lives; or you might not like each other at all. In the end, what really matters is your daughter's relationship to these people—and this is why you are extending yourself: To ease the path for her. We couldn't have said it any better than Ellen, a mother of three brides:

> "This is something I've thought a lot about. Being Jewish, I'm aware of a Yiddish word, 'mahatunim,' that refers to your relationship with your child's in-laws. I'm fascinated by the fact that no such word exists in English. I think having or not having that word indicates whether or not you have an expectation that these people (whom you may or may not like) will now be part of your extended family and they are people you actually do have a relationship 'to,' whether or not you choose to have a relationship 'with' them. I think on one hand it's a time that can get stressful and it's easy to have difficult feelings. On the other hand, if you keep the planning in perspective and remember that these are people your daughter will have to live her life among, you'll want to make sure things go as smoothly as possible, and maybe the excitement of all the plans makes this a very easy time to get to know and like them— sort of a honeymoon period for the families! I have been fortunate not to have difficult situations, but I think it would be important not to do anything that will make life more difficult or complicated for your daughter, or for your new son-in-law."

Now that's mother wisdom as good as we've ever heard it.

Averting Culture Clashes

Cultural differences can not only happen when your daughter is marrying a man from a different country, it can happen within your own country, even your own city. Cultural differences can be religious-, ethnic-, or class-based. They can occur between people who are from urban and rural areas. They can occur between carnivores and vegetarians! Cultural differences are as potentially numerous as the flowers in your daughter's bouquet.

Keepsakes

"When Deb married Luc, six or eight people traveled here from Belgium. This was somewhat of a different situation. The family arrived several days before the wedding and planned to stay several days afterward. The language was a problem since they spoke no English and I spoke no French. Luc's father came prepared with a French-English dictionary, which we used constantly. We also did a lot of sign language so we managed okay. We had a lot of fun through it all. It was important to Deb and Luc to combine customs and traditions from the United States as well as Belgium. I think they accomplished that goal."

—Jane, mother of brides Debra and Christina

That's okay. Differences are good. They're what keep us interesting and enrich our lives with new experiences. With that said, differences can also be pretty frustrating, and sometimes downright annoying. But whatever cultural differences you may have with your daughter's future in-laws, your ultimate goal is to keep relations smooth, or as smooth as they can be.

What follows are some suggestions for handling your differences:

- Be aware of your feelings. It's far better to fess up (to yourself!) about any uncomfortable, threatened, or angry feelings you have so that you can deal with them accordingly (instead of not dealing with them and blowing up at an inopportune moment).

- Ask questions. Don't understand a custom or a cultural difference? Ask about it. Instead of thinking to yourself, "That's strange," or "That's not what *we* do," learn why something is done and where that custom comes from. Understanding is the number-one way to combat fear and anger.

- Don't take it personally. Someone else's different customs or habits do not represent a rejection of your own.

- Try to see your differences as an opportunity to learn about a way of life different from your own, as well as a way to learn more about your future son-in-law.

- Share. This country is the melting pot, isn't it? So of course there's room for more than one way of doing things. Sharing your customs is a great way to get to know each other and make your daughter's in-laws comfortable. One mother of the bride whose Irish/Italian daughter was marrying a man of Indian descent had foods from her family's heritage as well as those of her son-in-law's at the engagement party she threw. Sharing your cultural history on the table is a great way to show respect for each other's customs.

Mother-in-Law of the Year

We've done a lot of talking about your future son-in-law's parents—but what about him? This young man is going to be an important part of your family from now on, so if you haven't already, now's the time to make some important ground rules and create a strong foundation for a good mother-in-law/son-in-law relationship.

Hopefully, you're fond of this young man, but even if you've gotten off to a bumpy start you can still mend what's broken. It's not easy watching your daughter put her heart in the care of someone you don't know very well. Will he be good to her? Will he hurt her? Who *is* this guy?!

That's exactly what you should find out. And, in turn, he'll get to know what makes you tick, too. Get to know his likes and dislikes, learn what makes him tick and what's important to him. Learn what makes him laugh! Think about how your parents extended themselves—or didn't, as the case may be—to your own husband when you got married.

Keepsakes

"I believe we act in a particular way as a reaction to our past experiences. Your questions conjured up memories of forty-two years ago, when my opinions of planning weddings were formed. I was the last child to 'leave' my parents, and my father was so saddened by this thought that he allowed no discussion of my wedding in his presence. He gave [my husband] his permission to marry me, and that was the end of his participation … I decided then, that if I ever had children who wanted to get married, their weddings would be their weddings."

—Theresa, mother of bride Charlotte and groom Tom

If you always treat your son-in-law like the enemy at the gate, he'll never feel comfortable in your home and, therefore, neither will your daughter. At best you'll see less of them than you'd like; at worst you could do damage to her marriage. This is the

man your daughter loves and who she has chosen
to spend her life with. You must respect this. As an
adult, she has made this decision and you should
support her in it, by …

- Always making her and her husband feel
  welcome in your home. He is family now
  and should be treated as such.

- Respecting their decisions, even when you
  don't agree with them.

- Offering advice and counsel, but never med-
  dling or nagging them to do what you want
  or feel is best.

- Not being rigid about adopting new family
  traditions. Your daughter and her husband
  are trying to form their new life together,
  and that may well mean that some old pat-
  terns and customs might change. While this
  might not always be easy to accept, it's part
  of how a family grows—and subsequently
  stays together.

- Communicating and being clear. Don't use
  passive-aggressive techniques to try to sway
  your son-in-law to your way of thinking. If
  something is important to you, say what's on
  your mind, have an adult discussion, and
  honor the conclusion you both come to.

Wediquette

Save your son-in-law the awkwardness of figuring out what to call you once he marries your daughter—sit down and talk about it beforehand. Tell him what you're comfortable with and ask him what he would prefer. If you'd like him to call you "mom," but he doesn't feel okay with that, then first names are fine. Just make sure you broach the topic before the wedding and you come to a mutual decision. That way, he won't feel awkward and you won't wonder why he always refers to you as, "Ummmm …"!

Chapter 7

Standing on Ceremony

In This Chapter

- Handling the ceremony planning
- Ways to incorporate your family's cultural traditions into the ceremony
- Receiving line etiquette

Sometimes the actual wedding can be overshadowed by the hullabaloo that surrounds the wedding reception. Think back, though, to your own wedding—the feeling of anticipation; how big and slightly surreal the moment felt when you walked down the aisle toward your husband-to-be standing at the altar of your church or stood together moments before the justice of the peace began to read the words that would unite you and begin a whole new chapter of your life. This declaration of love and commitment in front of those near and dear is the nexus of the whole day—and the commencement of your daughter's new chapter in her own life.

If you have chosen to take on the ceremony arrangements for your daughter's day, this chapter will give you the basics on what you need to do, who you need to pay, and how to make sure the ceremony is as meaningful and lovely as you know she wants it to be. We'll also talk a little about handling differences of opinion on ceremonial matters, different ethnic and cultural traditions that your daughter and her fiancé may want to add to personalize the nuptials, and, finally, who goes where in the receiving line afterward.

Discussing the Ceremony with Your Daughter

Of course, even if you're taking on the duty of planning the ceremony, your daughter will be a big part of the planning. You will want and need her input every step of the way. The ceremony can bring up strong feelings about culture, tradition, and personal belief systems. It's important to recognize that, as an adult, your daughter may or may not embrace the religious belief system in which she was raised. If she does, then you can both get right to the nitty-gritty of where and when.

If not, you should probably have a sit-down about this important aspect of the wedding. Don't assume your daughter envisions the same ceremony that you do. Make a date to get together and discuss what she envisions for the ceremony. If it's different from what you expected, it will be easier for you to discuss this together calmly than assume you're in sync on this issue. You don't want to find out, when you happily announce that you've secured your local priest, that your daughter plans on having an outdoor civil ceremony.

Wediquette

Ethnic and cultural traditions and rites can be very important in a family. There are many ways to incorporate these traditions into a wedding, even if the ceremony does not follow the exact religious or cultural ceremony blow by blow. See the Ceremony Culture Table in this chapter for suggestions on how to incorporate various ethnic and cultural traditions of your family and your future son-in-law into the big day.

It might be difficult to learn or acknowledge that your daughter doesn't follow the religious system in which you have raised her, or that she's embracing the religious system of her fiancé. (Keep in mind that if your future son-in-law is embracing yours, his parents will go through this same dilemma.) Of course, you should feel absolutely within your bounds to calmly discuss this with her. Learn her thoughts on the matter and share your own. It's important as mother and daughter to discuss this issue so there's a basic understanding of why each of you feels the way she does.

However, in the end, this is your daughter's wedding and she is an adult who is able to make serious decisions on her own. Do not try to force the issue. You want her to remember this day as full of love, happiness, and positive feelings—not the day that she compromised something of great importance to her, or that she stuck to her guns and her mother sat and frowned through the whole day.

Keepsakes

"My daughter-in-law and her family had a Brahmin do a one-hour form of the Hindu ceremony, and my son asked my brother to read marriage vows from our traditional ceremony."

—Theresa, mother of bride Charlotte and groom Tom

The Basics of Planning a Ceremony

With that said, let's get down to the planning. What follows is a checklist to get you and your daughter on your way to planning the ceremony:

- Pick a date. Once your daughter and her fiancé settle on a day, you can get to work on the details—so the sooner they get out their calendars, the better!

- Discuss with your daughter what kind of ceremony she plans on having (religious, secular, in church, outdoors, city hall, etc.).

- Secure the officiant, the ceremony site, and
  the officiant's attendance at the rehearsal the
  day before the wedding. If your daughter
  intends to marry in your or her local synagogue or church, the officiant can tell you
  what dates and times are available, as well as
  the time allotted for the length of the ceremony. If she plans to be married in a location other than where the officiant generally
  does his or her job, you will need to coordinate and secure the ceremony spot as well.
  Do this early! The earlier you start, the more
  options you'll have.

- Find out how much the fee is for the officiant's services as well as the cost of reserv-
  ing the site.

- If the ceremony is Christian, find out if
  there is a church organist, choir, or something similar, to provide music.

- Regardless of the denomination, make sure
  there aren't any restrictions placed on singers,
  number of musicians, or musical selection at
  the site before hiring these vendors.

- Find out if there are restrictions on flowers,
  decorations, and the like at the site. If there
  has been a particular holiday and the site is
  already decorated, ask if you can use those
  decorations to save some money.

- If your daughter prefers a religious ceremony and is marrying someone outside her
  faith, find out if any issues or paperwork
  need to be taken care of beforehand.

- If your daughter prefers a religious ceremony and is marrying outside of her parish church, find out if there is any paperwork that she needs to provide to her new church.

- Find out from the officiant how long the service generally runs so you can coordinate music and readings, and, if Christian, whether your daughter wishes to include a full mass or just the ceremony.

- Figure out how many guests the ceremony site can accommodate as well as whether the site has adequate parking.

- Make sure the officiant has the proper spelling and (more importantly) pronunciation of your daughter's name and the name of her fiancé.

- Find out if the ceremony site allows the tossing of rose petals or birdseed after the ceremony.

- Will a podium or chuppah be provided by the site, or will you have to bring this yourself?

- Are there any restrictions on photography?

- Are there any restrictions on attire?

After you have all the pertinent questions answered, your daughter settles on a date, and you secure the site and the officiant, make sure you follow up and confirm the date, time, and officiant and, if possible, get the terms of your agreement in writing.

Wediquette

Deciding on the music and how much to have can be a dilemma. Of course, find out from your daughter and her fiancé if there are particular songs or a type of music that's special to them and that they'd prefer. Usually, you will need about two or three songs before the service (when guests are being seated), and two to four during the ceremony, depending on how extensive the service is. Songs should never last for more than three to five minutes.

Adding Cultural Touches

There are many reasons to personalize a ceremony with the cultural traditions of the bride and groom. For one, it adds a special, individual touch to the service and signifies the joining of their backgrounds. It also can be a way to compromise. If you and your daughter have different ideas about how the ceremony will play out, adding cultural details from your family's background can bridge the gap between old traditions and new.

Following, we've listed some wedding ceremony traditions from a myriad of cultural backgrounds. See if one or two of them fit with your daughter and her fiancé's vision for their day.

Ceremony Culture Table

Country/Culture/Religion	Tradition
African American	An individual special to the bride and groom places a broom in the path of the newlyweds, which the couple jump over on the way out. It symbolizes the beginning of their new domestic life together.
	The bride and groom exchange wedding rings with the ankh symbol, which means eternal life.
Chinese	Often the bride wears red, as it is a symbol of love, happiness, and prosperity.
	The time of the ceremony is on the half-hour to symbolize the start of their life on an upswing.
	The groom goes first to the bride's home and they travel to the ceremony site together.
Czechoslovakian	Before the wedding, the bride's attendants plant a tree in her yard and decorate it with ribbons to bring long life to the bride.
	Just before the ceremony, a baby is placed on the couple's bed to bring fertility.
	Right after the ceremony, the bride's wedding veil is exchanged for a marriage bonnet to represent her move from maiden to married woman.

Country/Culture/ Religion	Tradition
Egyptian	Before vows are exchanged, a lively *zaffa* occurs, which is a processional of belly dancers, flaming swordsmen, and drummers and horns as part of the rousing music.
Filipino	In old traditional style, a Filipino bride wears her "best dress," which usually is of a bright color; the groom wears a *barong tagalog*, an almost translucent ecru-colored linen shirt with ornate embroidery on the front worn untucked with a white T-shirt underneath and black pants.
	Brides carry orange blossoms in their bouquets or in their hair.
	Traditional Filipino weddings involve several sets of sponsors, who perform particular duties throughout the ceremony (usually Catholic), a lovely way to involve several friends and relatives in the nuptials. Candle sponsors light the two candles that flank a larger center candle, which is the unity candle that the bride and groom light together; veil sponsors drape a sheer white veil over the head and shoulders of the bride and groom to represent the uniting of the couple; and cord sponsors loosely put a white cord around the necks of the couple in a figure 8 to represent the new bond between the bride and groom.

continues

Ceremony Culture Table   (continued)

Country/Culture/Religion	Tradition
	The groom gives the bride 13 coins in a promise to take care of the bride.
French	The groom meets the bride at her home and walks her to the church. Children follow the soon-to-be betrothed and throw white ribbons at them, which the bride collects and snips in half as she walks.
	The bride wears orange blossoms in her hair.
	Laurel leaves are scattered outside the church.
	Flowers with a very strong perfume are used in the bouquet to ward off evil spirits.
	The nuptials occur under a silk canopy called a *carre* to protect the bride and groom from bad luck.
	Coins are tossed to children after the ceremony.
German	In the traditional 3-day celebration, the first day the couple weds in a civil ceremony and on the third they have the religious ceremony.
	The bride carries salt and bread to symbolize a good harvest and the groom carries grain as a symbol of luck and prosperity.

Country/Culture/ Religion	Tradition
	The only attendant the bride has is a flower girl.
	The bride and groom kneel during the ceremony. In a show of who is to be the head of the household, the groom may kneel on top of the bride's train or skirt. When they stand, however, the bride may (gently!) step on the groom's foot to show she plans to head the household.
	The bride carries a white ribbon in her bouquet.
	Wedding rings are worn on the right hand, not the left.
	Rice is thrown at the bride and groom as they leave the ceremony and however many grains of rice stay in the bride's hair is how many children they will have.
	Coins are thrown to children.
Greek	The bride may carry either sugar, to represent a sweet life, or ivy, to represent never-ending love.
	The bride may wear a yellow or red veil. The colors represent fire, which is thought to protect her from evil spirits.

continues

Ceremony Culture Table (continued)

Country/Culture/ Religion	Tradition
	The bride and groom wear wreaths of gold or orange blossoms on their heads, which are tied together by a long silk ribbon.
Hungarian	The ceremony, part of the traditional three-day wedding celebration, occurs under a white tent.
	The bride gives her groom a lucky number of three or seven handkerchiefs and he gives her a bag of coins.
	After the ceremony, a *naszmenet*, or bridal procession, is led to the reception by an uncle of the bride.
Indian	The bride wears a bejeweled *sari* of red or gold and her hands and feet are painted with henna.
	Sweets, eggs, and money representing a good life, fertility, and prosperity are introduced into the ceremony.
	When the bride's father presents her to the groom, the groom ties a pendant around her neck to symbolize fidelity and happiness.
	A small ceremonial fire burns and the couple makes symbolic offerings to it. They are bound together with a sash and then walk around the fire seven times to symbolize their commitment to walk through life's challenges together.

Country/Culture/ Religion	Tradition
	The groom puts vermillion powder in the bride's hair to show that she is now a married woman.
Iranian	The groom purchases the bride's wedding dress, which features a 10-foot long piece of sheath that he wraps around her at the ceremony to symbolize her transition to a married woman.
	A woman who is happily married holds a see-through shawl over the couple's head.
	After the vows are exchanged, two ornamental sugar cones are crumbled and sprinkled over the new couple to symbolize good luck.
Irish	The bride may carry a horseshoe turned up for good luck.
	Chiming bells are used to keep evil spirits away and maintain harmony between the couple.
	The bride carries a special handkerchief that later can be made into a christening bonnet for the first baby. The child later carries it as a hanky on his/her own wedding day.

continues

Ceremony Culture Table   (continued)

Country/Culture/ Religion	Tradition
	An Irish bride might wear a blue dress or a dress with blue in it to represent good luck; no one, however, should wear green to the wedding because that is considered bad luck.
	The bride braids her hair because it is thought to help her hold on to feminine powers and luck.
	Claddagh rings—two hands (representing faith) that hold a heart (representing love) that wears a crown (representing honor)— can be used as the wedding rings. Make sure the top of the crown faces out (if the ring is turned the other way with the hands facing out, it means you're single!).
	Marrying on a Saturday is considered unlucky, but tossing a horseshoe over the bride's head when she leaves the church is supposed to bring luck to the couple.
Italian	The groom carries a piece of iron to ward off evil spirits; the bride wears a veil covering her face for the same purpose.
	A ribbon is tied in front of the church to symbolize the bonds of marriage.

Country/Culture/ Religion	Tradition
	Getting married on a Sunday is considered good luck, but wearing gold anytime before gold rings are exchanged at the ceremony is considered bad luck.
Japanese	The bride not only dresses in a white kimono and an ornamental headpiece, but also is painted white to symbolize her maiden status. The groom wears a black kimono.
	Nine cups of sake are drunk by the couple at the ceremony to secure their unity as a married couple.
Jewish	Both parents escort the bride down the aisle toward the chuppah, a canopy that symbolizes the tent homes that couples lived in during ancient times.
	Plain gold wedding rings are exchanged so that wealth does not lead them astray.
	The *ketubah* (marriage contract) is signed by the couple beforehand and then read aloud during the ceremony. It is given to the bride and groom after the ceremony ends.

continues

Ceremony Culture Table (continued)

Country/Culture/ Religion	Tradition
	Seven blessings are bestowed upon the bride and groom by someone special to them in the family.
	Ceremonial wine is sipped during the rites. After the final sip of wine is taken, the groom takes the empty glass, wraps it in a cloth, and sets it on the ground, where he then steps on it and breaks it. This is a symbol of the destruction of the temple in Jerusalem and demonstrates how delicate love is.
Mexican	The ceremony traditionally occurs at nine o'clock in the evening.
	A long rosary called a *lazo* is draped over both the bride and groom at the altar to represent their joining together.
	The groom gives the bride thirteen coins, which are blessed by the priest during the ceremony, as a symbol of commitment.
	Red beads are tossed at the newlyweds as they leave the church to symbolize good luck.

Country/Culture/ Religion	Tradition
Norwegian	The bride wears a gold and silver crown woven with little silver bangles, which make a tinkling noise that wards off evil spirits.
	Sterling silver rings are used in the ceremony.
	Fir trees can be used at the ceremony to signify fertility.
Polish	The bride's parents present the couple with salted rye bread and a glass of wine. The bread symbolizes fulfillment, the salt that life can sometimes be difficult, and the wine the hope that the bride and groom will never be thirsty and will have a life filled with joy.
South African	A candle representing their unity is lit by the bride and groom after the vows are taken.
	Several symbols of love and strength must be present at the ceremony, including wheat, wine, salt, pepper, bitter herbs, a pot, a spoon, water, honey, a spear, a shield, and the Koran or the Bible, depending upon their religious affiliation.
Spanish	The bride uses orange blossoms in her bouquet or wears them in her hair to represent fertility and happiness.

continues

Ceremony Culture Table (continued)

Country/Culture/Religion	Tradition
	Just before the ceremony, the groom gives the bride thirteen coins to signify his commitment to her. The bride puts the coins in a small pouch and carries them during the ceremony.
	Some Spanish brides wear a black dress and black lace veil, while the groom wears a shirt embroidered by the bride.
Swedish	Before leaving for the ceremony, the bride's father gives her a silver coin for her left shoe, and her mother a gold coin for the right shoe, symbolizing prosperity.
	A Swedish bride will wear three rings by the time the ceremony is through: one for her engagement, one for her marriage, and one for fertility.

Wediquette

Bring with you to the ceremony and reception an "emergency" wedding kit just in case your daughter happens to stumble upon a minor disaster: clear nail polish, safety pins, extra mascara and lipstick, spare contacts and solution (if she—and you!—wear them), a sewing kit, and nail file.

After the Ceremony

After the "I do's" have been said, the processional song commences, and the bride and groom glide down the aisle among the happy faces of their near and dear. The following is the traditional order of exiting for the rest of the immediate wedding party and family:

- flower girl and ring bearer
- maid of honor and best man
- bridesmaids accompanied by an usher
- the bride's parents
- the groom's parents
- the bride's grandparents
- the groom's grandparents
- wedding guests

After the recessional is done, the receiving line forms as follows:

- mother of the bride
- father of the bride
- mother of the groom
- father of the groom
- bride
- groom
- maid of honor
- bridesmaids

If you have remarried because your husband is deceased, obviously your husband will be next to you in the same order as above. If you and the bride's father are divorced and if either or both of you have remarried, the order is as follows:

- mother of the bride
- stepfather of the bride
- mother of the groom
- father of the groom
- stepmother of the bride
- father of the bride
- bride
- groom
- maid of honor
- bridesmaids (unless you think the line is too long at this point, and then it is acceptable to just have immediate family in the receiving line)

Of course, this is just a guide. You and your daughter should feel free to arrange the receiving line in whatever order makes you, her, and anyone else involved comfortable. However you decide to situate everyone, remember: The main point is to avoid having your daughter fret over potential hurt feelings or uncomfortable situations.

Chapter 8

Exceptional Receptions

In This Chapter

- Your role at the reception
- How to make your daughter's day hassle-free
- How to make sure you enjoy yourself!

So here it is—the Big Day. You and your daughter have spent months upon months making plans, going over the details, arranging and rearranging, and you've kept the bride calm, cool, and collected when you sensed she was becoming overwhelmed. The ceremony went off without a hitch (and, thankfully, you wore waterproof mascara and had a packet of tissues in your purse). Now it's time to celebrate. But hold on—you're not off-duty yet!

Hostess for a Day

As mother of the bride, you are the official hostess of the day. If you're shocked to learn this, don't feel too bad. The rules of weddings have changed quite a bit over the years to accommodate evolving attitudes and trends in society, and many of the "traditional" roles and duties have been altered, nixed, or just plain lost in the shuffle.

Keepsakes

"The daughter's personality has to be your guide. If she is easily persuaded, encourage her to make her own decisions. If she is strong and in total control, give an opinion only when asked, and gently. Be the calming effect, the stabilizer if possible. Listen, listen, and listen some more."

—Theresa, mother of bride Charlotte and groom Tom

But we think the role of hostess is an important one to hang on to for several reasons:

- In the dizzying, glorious, happy swirl of her wedding day, the bride may well not notice any number of details at her reception—a vendor who's not exactly fulfilling his or her duties, a DJ who hasn't eaten but was promised a meal in his or her contract, the hurt feelings of an aunt because she feels ignored. Your daughter needs her mom more than ever to keep her eagle eye on the details so that she remembers her wedding day with a smile, not an exasperated eye roll.

- Your daughter may be an international mover and shaker, but it is your wisdom and experience in your family and in the world that are going to be of the utmost use. The bride may be able to broker business deals in Japanese, but does she know that it's wise not to sit cousins Frank and Michael together because of a long-standing but hush-hush family feud?

● If you have arranged and paid for the wedding, you will be more than well-versed in the conditions of your contracts with each vendor and able to make sure all promises are fulfilled. Besides, should the bride really have to haggle with a photographer who's trying to cut out earlier than he's supposed to when she should be out on the floor dancing with her new husband?

Keepsakes

"My part of the reception seemed to go well. Since we were paying this particular bill, I was the liaison with the owner/manager. I instructed the still photographer. I tried to make sure everyone was having a good time. Advice? Concentrate on the bride and groom's happiness. Intervene only when something is totally unfair. Remember that you want a future, friendly relationship with your child, his/her spouse, and the in-laws."

—Theresa, mother of bride Charlotte and groom Tom

This is not to say that you should spend the entire day sweating all the details to the point of distraction. You've invested a lot of time and effort in helping your daughter and son-in-law put this fete together (not to mention *raising* the girl!). But what, exactly, should you do?

- Arrive at the reception early to prepare to greet the guests as they arrive and instruct them on where to go (where to find the assigned seating cards, where the cocktail hour is, where the dinner will be, where they can leave gifts if they brought them to the reception, and so on).

- Make sure vendors are where they should be and doing what they were hired to do. Also, assuming this is in their contract, make sure the vendors are fed during the reception (although, even if it isn't in their contract, it's the right thing to do).

- Dance with the groom at some point during the evening, but not before he dances with his own mother or step-mother.

- Walk around during the reception to make sure the guests are happy and comfortable.

- Be your daughter's guardian angel—make sure, of everyone there, that she and her fiancé are enjoying themselves and not bogged down with the logistics of the reception, petty family squabbles, or anything else that really is not relevant to the day.

- Know that nothing is ever perfect. By all means, try to put out any major fires that pop up during the reception, but do recognize that *something* is bound to not go exactly as you or your daughter had planned. And that's okay! The most important thing is the overall happiness of the bride and groom and those who are close to them.

Keepsakes

"I believed—and I think my daughters did, too—that, although this is an important occasion and you want it to go beautifully, you have to keep some perspective. Nothing is ever perfect and I don't think it's worth everyone's sanity to drive yourselves crazy seeking perfection. You make decisions that you feel are good, you find competent people to do the things they're hired to do, and then you try to relax and remember what this is all about—the beginning of a life together and a joyful celebration, not a royal coronation. If this is truly the happiest day of the bride's life, then why bother going on? It's a hugely important day, a wonderful day, but let's have a little reality check here!"

—Ellen, mother of brides Judith, Meg, and Debra

Your Daughter's Keeper

How can you help your daughter have a great day? First and foremost—and this might not be the advice you're expecting—enjoy yourself. You can't prevent mistakes or problems from happening. You *can* try to steer your daughter away from anything potentially upsetting, and we heartily encourage you to do so. But the sight of her mom with a furrowed brow and beads of sweat pouring down her face for six hours would likely upset her as much as the cake toppling to the floor. Remember: Don't sweat the small stuff.

It might seem like a pile of tasks we're throwing at you in this chapter, but the fact is you've already gone over all the details with the caterer and other vendors. Of course, it's possible something might not go exactly to your liking and you should keep an eye on them to make sure they're fulfilling their assigned and paid-for duties. Outside of that, your main task is to be the hostess with the mostest. Smile, dance, chat with the guests. (Hey, there are far worse jobs than this!)

One surefire thing you can do beforehand to head off any potential bridal trouble is to prepare an aesthetic emergency kit of sorts and stash it with your coat or purse. We know one bride who, while reaching her arms around her dad's shoulder to give him a big hug after their father-daughter dance, busted a spaghetti strap on her lovely silk wedding dress. Lucky for her, her mom came prepared with safety pins and hooked her back together before any guests could be the wiser. To keep bridal or bridesmaid (or mother of the bride or groom!) beauty issues in check, pack a little bag and fill it with:

- Small sewing kit
- Nail clipper
- Tweezer
- Clear nail polish
- Extra pantyhose
- Safety pins
- Pain reliever
- Tissues
- Visine
- Hair pins
- Translucent powder
- Deodorant
- Travel-size bottle/can of hairspray
- Travel-size bottle of mouthwash or breath mints
- Band-aid
- Neosporin
- Mascara

Many of these items have multiple uses other than the obvious (hair spray can also eliminate static cling; a nail clipper can cut stray threads; clear nail polish can stop a pantyhose run from running amuck). But no matter what the beauty snafu, with this kit you'll be prepared for (almost) anything.

Keepsakes _____

"There were a few disappointments with photographs and video, but we chose people who had excellent reputations and work samples, so there was no way that could have been helped. It's disappointing, but you just have to let go of it. In terms of the choices made on the ceremony and reception, etc., I look back on the three weddings with great pleasure, and I think my daughters also would not wish anything had been different."

—Ellen, mother of brides Judith, Meg, and Debra

Wedding Reception Traditions

Following, just like in the previous chapter, we've listed some wedding reception traditions from a diverse sampling of cultural backgrounds. See if your daughter and her fiancé would like to incorporate one or two into their day.

Reception Culture Table

Country/Culture/Religion	Tradition
Chinese	The bride changes into several outfits during the reception.

Country/Culture/ Religion	Tradition
	An announcer greets guests and begins the reception festivities.
	An elaborate, tall, multilayered cake is a large part of the reception as its height and layers represent the couple's successful future climb to success.
	The bride and groom first feed each other cake with their arms entwined, then the parents, grandparents, and so on are given a piece of the "good luck" cake.
Czechoslovakian	For the reception, the bride's wedding veil is exchanged for a marriage bonnet to represent her move from maiden to married woman.
	Guests of the bride and groom sing a special Czechoslovakian wedding song.
	Kolache is eaten, a traditional Czech wedding pastry usually made with fruit.
Egyptian	At the reception, the bride and groom sit in a *kosha*, two special seats reserved for the new couple where guests can greet them and they can act as "king and queen" of the festivities.

continues

Reception Culture Table (continued)

Country/Culture/ Religion	Tradition
	A rose sherbet drink is used for the toast, which occurs in the beginning of the reception, and the bride and groom move their wedding rings from their right index fingers to the left index fingers, symbolizing the official beginning of the reception.
	The traditional food of an Egyptian ceremony is the *Fattah*, lamb in rice and bread dipped in a stew.
	During the dancing, the groom is often tossed in the air by his friends. The more often he is tossed, the more well liked he is by those around him.
Filipino	The bride and groom engage in a special dance called the *Pandango*, where guests pin money to the couple to help pay for their honeymoon.
	The bride and groom cut the cake together, each take a bite separately, and then interlock elbows and simultaneously take a bite.
	During the first dance, the bride starts off dancing with her father and the groom with his mother, and then they switch so the new couple are given to each other and dance together.

Country/Culture/ Religion	Tradition
French	When the first toast is made to the bride and groom, the couple drink from a two-handled goblet called *la coupe de mariage*, which is often specially engraved for them.
	A special "cake" called a *croquembouche* is featured. It is made of small pastry puffs filled with cream, covered with glaze, and shaped like a pyramid.
	Sometimes guests also bring tiny cakes to the reception, which they stack on top of each other. The bride and groom are supposed to kiss over the top of it to ensure a long, happy life together.
	After the official reception, wedding guests are expected to engage in a *chiverie*, during which they show up at the bride and groom's home (or room, if in a hotel or inn), banging pots and singing songs until the couple invites them in for a drink and something to eat.
German	In the traditional three-day celebration, the second day is when the celebratory reception is held, called the *polterabend*.

continues

Reception Culture Table (continued)

Country/Culture/ Religion	Tradition
	For good luck, guests bring old dishes to the party and break them on the floor to scare away evil spirits. Afterward, the bride and groom sweep them up as a symbol of everything being in its place in their new home and nothing ever being broken again.
	Hochzeitssuppe, a traditional wedding soup made of beef, dumplings, and vegetables, is part of the menu.
Greek	The bride and groom dance the traditional dance called the *kalamatiano*, during which each holds an end of the same scarf.
	White-coated almonds called *koufeta* are given to wedding guests as a symbol of the simultaneous sweetness and bitterness of life. An odd number should be counted for each gift, though, as it represents good luck.
	Guests dance with the bride and groom and pin money to the couple's clothes.
Hungarian	As guests arrive at the reception, they are offered a drink of *palinka*, a strong Hungarian brandy usually consumed as a shot.
	It is common to serve Hungarian goulash and stuffed cabbage.

Country/Culture/ Religion	Tradition
	The bride dances the *menyasszony-tanc*, a traditional wedding dance during which guests pay to dance with the bride—and the price goes up with each dance!
Iranian	The post-nuptial celebratory party, called the *Aroosi*, is marked by a lavish meal. Central to it is often a whole roasted lamb and two kinds of rice, *Morrasah Polo* ("jeweled" rice) and *Shirin Polo* (sweet rice).
Irish	The traditional Irish post-nuptial feast is held at the bride's parents' home.
	Guests may race from the church to the reception.
	Mead, a type of wine made from honey, water, and yeast, is consumed by the bride and groom and guests.
	A rich cake made of fruit is the traditional Irish wedding cake served to guests. The top tier, however, is a "whiskey cake," which should be saved for the christening of the couple's first child.
Italian	An Italian bride and groom will often walk through their town after the nuptials to the ceremony, greeting everyone in their town as husband and wife.

continues

Reception Culture Table   (continued)

Country/Culture/ Religion	Tradition
	The food at an Italian wedding is central to the celebration. Many courses, including antipasto, pastas, and meats, may be served throughout the reception.
	It is good luck to serve bow tie–shape twists of fried dough covered with powdered sugar and candy-coated almonds, which represent the sweet and bitter aspects of life.
	The *tarantella*, a traditional Italian dance, is often performed by guests.
	Before the end of the reception, the bride and groom break a glass. The amount of pieces that shatter represent the many years of happiness that the couple will have together.
	An honored male guest will give the toast, *"Eviva gli sposi!"* or, "Hurray for the newlyweds!" and the rest of the guests respond with clapping and cheering. This toast happens not just once, but throughout the reception.
Japanese	The bride changes into a red kimono for the first part of the reception, and later into a Western dress.
	Guests give *goshugi*, a wedding gift of money in a decorative envelope.

Country/Culture/ Religion	Tradition
	While facing their guests, the couple lights a tall candle on the center table, which symbolizes their unity in marriage.
	The mother of the bride and mother of the groom traditionally receive a bouquet of flowers, while the fathers are given a carnation for the lapel of their jackets as a gesture of thanks.
Jewish	After the nuptials and prior to the ceremony, the bride and groom may go off to a room alone to perform a ritual called *yibun*, or union. Here they will sit alone and eat a simple soup together.
	If it is your only or last daughter who is being married, it is tradition to perform a *krenzl*: seat the mother of the bride in the center of the room and have her daughter or daughters crown her with flowers and dance around her chair.
	The newly married couple and their guests dance the *hora*. During this dance, the couple are each seated in a chair and hold a handkerchief between them. They are hoisted into the air by male guests, while the rest of the celebrants join hands and dance in a circle around them.

continues

Reception Culture Table   (continued)

Country/Culture/ Religion	Tradition
	A celebratory meal called a *seudah mitzfah* is eaten, and is followed by a recitation of after-meal grace, or *birkat hamazon*.
Mexican	Rice, beans, and tortilla dishes are traditional foods served at a Mexican reception. Sangria, a wine punch made with fresh fruit, is also served.
	A piñata holding candy hangs from the ceiling at the reception and is broken open by the children attending.
	When the bride and groom dance together for the first time, their guests surround them and form the shape of a heart, so their first dance is surrounded by love.
Norwegian	A rolling pin is passed around during the reception and signed by the guests as a keepsake for the couple.
Polish	When they enter the reception, the bride and groom are greeted by their parents who present them with a rye bread sprinkled with salt and wine. The rye bread is the parents' wish that their children will never go hungry; the salt is to acknowledge that life can be difficult; and the wine represents happiness for the couple.

Country/Culture/ Religion	Tradition
	The traditional money dance, where guests pin money to the bride's dress or toss it in an apron held by the maid of honor to "pay" for a twirl around the dance floor with the bride, is often performed.
	After the dance, the male guests form a tight circle around the bride that the groom must break through in order to claim his beloved.
	Upon entering the reception hall, the *oczepiny* ceremony is performed. This is when the bride's veil is removed to represent her movement from a maid to a married woman. The groom gets to wear a funny hat to signify that the marriage will be rich with happiness.
	If the bride can sip wine at her reception and not spill even a drop, it is considered lucky.
South African	After the wedding, the couple's parents carry kindling from their home to the home of the newly-weds to represent the beginning of their new life together.
Spanish	A dance called the *sequidilla manchega* is performed, where guests dance with the bride and give her money.

continues

Reception Culture Table (continued)

Country/Culture/ Religion	Tradition
	The wedding cake is often made of several cakes put together on a spiral stand, usually sponge cakes with a caramel topping and fresh cream or sponge cake filled with cherries and almonds and laced with rum. Cutting the cake is usually performed by the bride and groom with a special sword.
	A popular main course at a Spanish wedding is *Paella Valenciana*, a delicious, fragrant saffron rice dish with chicken, sausages, and seafood. Sangria is often served to drink with it.
	The bride may carry around a set of pins that resemble lilies or orchids and pass them out to all the unmarried women, who will wear them upside down while dancing. If the pin falls out, the woman will marry soon.
	The bride and groom may also go around the room and present each guest with a gift. The groom gives cigars to the men and the bride gives something sweet-smelling to the women.
Swedish	The Swedish wedding feast is usually dominated by the smorgasbord, a buffet of Swedish foods. In particular, the *brundlaupskling*, a Swedish sweet bread, is often featured.

Mother, Enjoy Thyself

As we said earlier in this chapter, if your daughter sees you carrying the weight of the wedding world on your shoulders, she won't be as joyful as she could be. And you certainly won't be, either. All that time and energy you and your daughter put into planning this day wasn't so you could grimace all afternoon and evening—it was so you and yours could celebrate this joyous occasion.

The day before the wedding, lay out your clothes, shoes, make-up, and various other accoutrements that you'll need so you won't have to fish through drawers and cabinets for this or that on the big day. Then set aside some "me" time. Go for a long walk or jog in your favorite park, see a movie, get a massage, go for a swim. Do whatever it is you like to do to relax and reflect. You deserve it for a job well done, and we don't just mean planning a wedding. We mean for being such a great mom.

Chapter 9

Nuclear (Family) Disarmament

In This Chapter

- Dealing with divorce
- Checking in with the father of the bride
- Family squabbles
- Helping to calm and counsel a nervous bride

As many good feelings as weddings bring out, there are a host of not-so-good feelings that can bubble to the punch-bowl surface. Petty family squabbles erupt or re-erupt, jealousy rears its ugly head, dad becomes disgruntled over losing his "little girl," awkward social situations arise courtesy of a past divorce. Sometimes you might be right smack in the middle of an ooey-gooey issue; sometimes you might just be an unfortunate observer.

In this chapter, we're going to look at some potential family minefields, and help you dismantle them with the ease and expertise of a professional bomb squad.

Le Divorce

You've heard the statistic: The divorce rate in the U.S. hovers at or above 50 percent. It's cited so often that not being aware of it is like not knowing your child's name. It means that at least half of you reading this book are no longer married to your daughter's father, or her stepfather, or her second stepfather. Or maybe you never remarried but *he* did, and he's bringing his second wife (or third or fourth) to the wedding. Whatever the situation, the upshot is you're not together anymore as your daughter's parental unit.

Of course, this might all be absolutely fine for you and your ex. Maybe enough years have gone by that all bad feelings have been worked out or left in the past. Maybe you're even good friends now, or at least on friendly terms. If so, we congratulate you (and maybe your therapist?) on a job well done. If not, then this wedding may well be causing some anxiety in your camp.

If you and your ex are not on Bruce-and-Demi terms, that's okay. Nobody said you had to like each other 'til death do you part. But what you do have to do is be civil to each other at the wedding. Period. There's no way around it. No comments under the breath, no eye-rolling, no tight smiles (at least not in front of your daughter). This isn't the time or place to air unresolved hostility. It *is* the place to celebrate what a beautiful child you made together. Hopefully, he will love and care as much about his daughter's happiness as you, but if he's not in the frame of mind he should be in:

Keepsakes _____

"There are so many mothers-of-the-bride who are divorced. Absolutely the feelings of the bride should be first and foremost on this day. Almost all of the time the parents should be able to be civil and get along for the sake of the bride. There are many ways of handling the formalities. The bride must again be creative. When Deb got married, both [my ex-husband and I] escorted the bride down the aisle. When Christina got married her father escorted her. Parents can dance together at the reception or with their current spouse or significant other or no formal dance at all. Mainly, talk with your bride daughter and see how she feels about this situation and let her know how you feel."

—Jane, mother of brides Debra and Christina and groom Tom

- As they say in Scotland, take the high road. Don't allow old, bad feelings to get the best of you and cause a scene on a day that really should be focused on the couple's happiness and the celebration of family.

- Smile, greet each other, and then go be with the people with whom you are each most comfortable. You don't have to pretend to be best buddies—in fact, do everyone a favor and don't. Just enjoy the lovely adult woman you created together, and then enjoy yourselves—separately.

- Use some pre-wedding strategizing. If you have a bad relationship with your ex-husband, try to make things as easy on yourself and him as possible. Designate seating arrangements in the church and at the reception ahead of time so that you are not stuck in the same pew or at the same table or adjacent ones.

- If you feel nervous and ill-at-ease at the notion of spending an entire day or evening in the same room as your ex, designate a lifesaver: Someone to stick by you and make sure that you're not involved in any awkward moments or situations that could potentially make you angry or upset or just uncomfortable. *This buddy should not be the bride!* It should, however, be a trusted friend, sibling, or cousin who knows the story and is sensitive to the situation.

- Scout out a breather place. While it might be your instinct to run into the ladies' room to have an emotional outpouring, we would advise against that as it could lead to an awkward meeting (your ex-husband's new wife, your former in-laws, your daughter) and an even more awkward explanation as to why you just kicked a toilet bowl. Find a quiet spot away from the festivities where you can take a deep breath and compose yourself.

When Daddy Loses His Little Girl

If you and your daughter's father are still married, you may have noticed some strange changes in his behavior. Moodiness, grumpiness, bouts of sullenness. Or maybe he's suddenly dressing like a man half his age and chatting with the groomsmen about extreme snowboarding. Who is this man?

Ah, don't you recognize him? He's the father of the bride—one who's having a little trouble coming to terms with his daughter's impending nuptials. Of course, not all dads express their ambivalence about a child's wedding in such extreme ways, but most are bound to have some emotional ups and downs to even out. How can you help?

Talk about it. Start a dialogue about your own feelings on the wedding to draw him out and allow him to get some of this off his chest. He might not know how to bring it up or talk about it; he might be worried that if he does he'll sound like one of those ogre parents who don't want to let their kids out into the world until they're at least 30 (even if, secretly, you both wish that were true!).

So help the guy out. If bringing up your own feelings isn't enough, then ask him right out. Is it hard on him at all? How does he feel? What's worrying him? You are each other's allies in this white storm known as your daughter's wedding. It's not easy to watch your children turn into adults—but it is a joy to realize what a good job you've done together.

Keepsakes

"Each wedding had its own emotional overlay. The first, of course, was the first, with all the implications about the change in the structure of our family, aging/mortality issues, etc. For the second, my husband was ill and that lent an added dimension, and the third wedding was after he had died, so, of course, there was a lot of emotion around that. Yes, of course there were difficult parts of each of those. Having a child marry, under any circumstances, is a huge emotional moment and I think it would be a mistake to not recognize and be prepared for that. I think it's those emotionally dramatic points of our lives that make our lives richer and fuller and, even if we have difficult emotional reactions, we need those reactions to remind us we're alive."

—Ellen, mother of brides Judith, Meg, and Debra

Family Feuds

Sadly, there's nothing like a wedding to bring out the bad side of certain family members. Thank goodness most of us realize that the time and the place to throw on the gloves and get in the ring is *not* during the cake cutting. But some folks just see any face-time as opportunity for a black eye. Or just to complain a lot.

We know one bride whose wedding began with a drunken phone call from her stepmother at 10 A.M., two hours before the wedding. There was also an angry message from a disgruntled sister, an uncle with Alzheimer's who spent the reception banging his fists on a table angry at a waiter, and an aunt who set her mouth in a grim line and complained during the whole wedding about how left out she felt.

Luckily, the bride had two fantastic allies in her camp: her mom and her cousin. While they couldn't shield the bride from all of the family kookiness that ensued, they were able to placate the sister, find a quiet spot for the uncle to rest and calm down, and ask the DJ to dedicate a special song for the aunt and have each of the men in the family dance with her. Pretty fast thinking.

To avert any family member's attempt to use your daughter's wedding as a place to air old grievances, follow the wedding buddy advice above and designate one or two trusted members of your family to keep an eye out for trouble and guide potential combatants to opposite corners. Chances are you are well versed in who's mad at whom and can even give out assignments. And of course, don't sit the disgruntled at the same table. The best way to stay out of trouble is to avoid it all together.

The Nervous Bride

She's cranky. She's distracted. She's weepy. She's ornery. She looks a bit like a deer in headlights. Does any of this sound familiar? They're classic symptoms of the bridus nervousitus.

If she's deeply involved in the planning there's a lot to be nervous about. Likely, she's never been part of planning a party this large before and there are a million and one details to worry over; her job pressure is mounting because she hasn't put in any extra time and is leaving for a two-week honeymoon vacation and the boss wants everything ship-shape before she leaves; she suddenly thinks she's picked the wrong dress; her bridesmaids are being pains in the butt; her ex-boyfriend suddenly started e-mailing her out of the blue (well, probably after he saw her wedding announcement in the paper). And, oh yes, she's getting married.

It's a lot to take in all at once, and anyone who's ever gotten married, even the calmest of women, knows that you can get pretty stressed out over the details. If this is what you think is making your daughter a nervous wreck, just do what you do best: Be there for her. Be her moral support, her shoulder-rubber, her champion. That is what she needs and that is what she needs you, the most important woman in her life, to do for her.

Keepsakes

"Charlotte has told me it's my job to keep her calm. This is no easy task, because I don't exactly know how to do it. If I agree too often, I'm placating. If I disagree, I don't understand. If I ask questions, I'm making her nervous. If I don't ask questions, I'm not interested. I'm 'winging it' all the time. How? Love, patience, self-sacrifice, hugs. My duties are:

- to be the moral support
- to pay the bills
- to be available whenever I'm needed
- to keep the 'annoying people' away from her
- to focus my attentions on her needs
- whatever comes up!"

—Theresa, mother of bride Charlotte and groom Tom

When the Problem Is More Than Nerves

You know better than anyone when something's *really* bothering your daughter. If she seems more than just a bit on edge, the problem might be bigger than party panic; it might be doubts about her decision of life partner.

So what do you do? There's a heartbreaking scene in the movie *The Wedding Singer* where the character Julia is trying on her wedding dress and bursts into tears—not over a bad fashion decision, but because of serious doubts about her fiancé. Her mother enters the room and although Julia says she has doubts, the mother discerns that her outburst is simply a case of wedding jitters; not that her daughter doesn't love the man she's about to marry.

Of course, this is just a movie, and a very light-hearted one at that (it's an Adam Sandler flick, for heaven's sake!), but the scene demonstrates an important issue, especially in a country where one in two couples on average will get divorced. It's very, very easy to feel pressured into marrying. Your daughter might be responding to any number of weighty real or perceived demands:

- She has been dating her fiancé for many years and sees this as the next "logical step" in the relationship, even though they may have grown up and grown apart and the actual next logical step is to break up. It may feel safer and less scary to her to stay with this young man (or woman), than to change her life and start fresh.

- Many of her friends, cousins, and/or colleagues are now married and she feels a certain social pressure to join the flock.

- Her significant other is pressuring her to tie the knot.

- She's worried she won't find anyone else.
- You, your husband, and the rest of the family are extremely fond of her fiancé and he's already treated as a family member.

These and any other number of reasons could be forcing your daughter into a decision that she doesn't want to make. So what do you do? What you do best: Talk to her. If some delicate general prodding doesn't give her the green light to express her true feelings, then be simultaneously direct and gentle. Ask her straight out: Are you happy with this decision? Do you feel you might be making a mistake? Open the door for her, because she might feel she can't do it herself.

Keepsakes

"I think my main contribution was in encouraging them to follow their instincts and to enjoy their weddings. That sounds simplistic, but they were mature and confident, so it left me to cheer them on."

—Helen, mother of brides Amy and Suzanne

Your greatest responsibility to your daughter is to be her advocate and to keep her safe. When she was a child, the latter meant childproofing the house and getting her safely to and from school.

As an adult, it means supporting her emotionally. Yes, it stinks that the dress was final-sale; that the invitations are out and RSVPs in; that the deposit on the catering hall is nonrefundable. That's all a big, fat inconvenience. But you know what's worse? Wedding yourself to someone you don't want to spend your life with, because the years you spend with a person you don't love are nonrefundable, too.

So talk to her. Maybe it's just nerves and she just needs someone to remind her to take a deep breath and coax a smile out of her. But if it's more than that, you might just be the one person who can help her not to make a very big mistake. You'd much rather give your daughter the opportunity to say she thinks she's made a mistake *before* the wedding than years after.

As the Bells Chime …

If you have made it to this part of the book, you're probably just about to watch that gorgeous, clever, assured woman you call your daughter walk down the aisle and begin a new chapter in her lovely life. It's been quite a ride, hasn't it? Soon enough, you'll be able to stop waking in the middle of the night with a jolt thinking, "Did I call the caterer back? Did that favor person say she'd wrap the wedding favors or that we'd have to do it ourselves? Did my daughter say her fiancé wants beef Wellington or well-done beef?" Your schedule will go back to normal; your cell phone will stop ringing like mad; you won't have to have any more annoying conversations with Aunt Gertrude about how she *still* thinks you made a mistake when you married your husband thirty some-odd years ago. Order will be restored to your home. Calm will return to your daily goings-on.

But maybe, sometimes, you'll find yourself wondering: Did I do a good job? Was my daughter happy? Was this the way she dreamed her wedding would be? When you find yourself mulling over these questions, pull out the photos from that great day. Look at her smiling face, the love in the eyes of her spouse, the tears of joy at the ceremony. And wait, isn't that grumpy Aunt Gertrude in the background cracking a smile?

There were probably a few things that went "wrong" during the ceremony or reception. But look again at those photos—it doesn't appear that anyone's thinking about how the florist brought the wrong color lilies or that the filet of sole was a bit overdone. They look like they're having the time of their lives. More importantly, the pure happiness on your daughter's face tells you all you need to know. You've done a great job—not just as a party planner extra-ordinaire, but as someone who loves that young woman as only her mother can. Congratulations, Mom. Your little girl is all grown up.

Wedding Planning Worksheets

Whether you're taking on all the planning duties or a few, you need to keep track of it all. What follows is a planner chock-full of checklists, reminders, and spaces for notes to keep whatever responsibilities you've taken on orderly and organized. Write in the book, or photocopy these pages (you might need or want extra pages than are provided here) and keep them in a loose-leaf notebook.

Timeline

Six Months to One Year Before:

- Arrange for a celebratory/get-to-know-you dinner or other social meeting with your daughter's future in-laws.
- Arrange and throw an engagement party.

- Figure out what you want to pay for and what you can afford, and make a budget accordingly.
- Find out from your daughter and her fiancé what type of wedding they wish to have (formal, semi-formal, casual).
- Help your daughter and her fiancé scout locations for the ceremony and reception, and reserve the final choice for the wedding day.
- Arrange transportation for the wedding party.
- Make your part of the guest list and gather your daughter's, her fiancé's, and his family's lists as well.
- Help your daughter decide upon and book the necessary professional services:
  - caterer
  - baker (if cake is not included in the above)
  - music for ceremony and reception
  - florist
  - photographer and videographer
- Shop for your daughter's dress as well as your own and set dates for fittings.

Four to Six Months Before:

- Go over the final guest list with your daughter.
- Order invitations and thank-you notes.

- Help your daughter and her fiancé register for gifts at a bridal registry.
- Book the bridal suite for the wedding night.
- Research hotels and inns near the reception and block out rooms for out-of-town guests.
- Send out "save the date" cards if you plan to.
- If need be, pick a day and location for the wedding shower, or offer assistance to the attendant throwing the shower.

Two Months Before:

- Mail invitations.
- Order or make favors for the wedding reception.
- Finalize/confirm arrangements with all wedding vendors.
- Schedule hair/nail/etc. salon appointments for yourself and, if needed, your daughter.

One Month Before:

- Purchase your daughter and future son-in-law's wedding gift.
- Attend final fitting for your daughter.
- Have your final fitting if necessary.
- Confirm accommodation reservations for out-of-town guests.

One Week Before:

- Get final guest count to caterer.

The Day Before:

- Attend rehearsal dinner.

The Wedding Day:

- Help your daughter get dressed.
- Make sure you have your checkbook or credit card for final fees due; bring cash for tips as well.
- Tell your daughter how beautiful she looks and how proud you are of the woman she's become.
- Have a great time!

Budget

Below is a list of traditionally expected wedding items, as well as others that you may or may not be footing the bill for. Whether you're paying for all or part of these items or a few of them, this worksheet is where you will record your budget so you can (hopefully!) stick to it:

Amount allotted for …

Engagement party: $ _____

Engagement gift: $ _____

Wedding dress and accoutrements: $ _____

Your dress and accoutrements: $ _____

Invitations: $ _____

Wedding programs: $ _____

Flowers: $ _____

Officiant: $ _____

Music for ceremony: $ _____

Reception: $ _____

Favors: $ _____

Band/DJ: $ _____

Cake: $ _____

Photographer: $ _____

Videographer: $ _____

Limousines/transportation: $ _____

Lodging for out-of-town family: $ _____

Wedding gift: $ _____

Honeymoon: $ _____

Engagement Party Guest List

Date: _____

Time: _____

Name of guest: _____
Relation to bride: (i.e., family, friend, groom's family)

_____

Attending: Yes ❑ No ❑

Name of guest: _____
Relation to bride: (i.e., family, friend, groom's family)

_____

Attending: Yes ❑ No ❑

Name of guest: _____
Relation to bride: (i.e., family, friend, groom's family)

_____

Attending: Yes ❑ No ❑

Name of guest: _____
Relation to bride: (i.e., family, friend, groom's family)

_____

Attending: Yes ❑ No ❑

Name of guest: _____
Relation to bride: (i.e., family, friend, groom's family)

_____

Attending: Yes ❑ No ❑

Name of guest: _____
Relation to bride: (i.e., family, friend, groom's family)

_____

Attending: Yes ❑ No ❑

Name of guest: _____
Relation to bride: (i.e., family, friend, groom's family)

_____

Attending: Yes ❑ No ❑

Name of guest: _____
Relation to bride: (i.e., family, friend, groom's family)

_____

Attending: Yes ❑ No ❑

Name of guest: _____
Relation to bride: (i.e., family, friend, groom's family)

_____

Attending: Yes ❑ No ❑

Name of guest: _____
Relation to bride: (i.e., family, friend, groom's family)

_____

Attending: Yes ❑ No ❑

Name of guest: _____
Relation to bride: (i.e., family, friend, groom's family)

_____

Attending: Yes ❑ No ❑

Name of guest: _____
Relation to bride: (i.e., family, friend, groom's family)

_____

Attending: Yes ❑ No ❑

Name of guest: _____
Relation to bride: (i.e., family, friend, groom's family)

_____

Attending: Yes ❑ No ❑

Wedding Guest List

We recommend that you photocopy this page as needed for the number of guests your daughter has invited to her wedding.

Name of guest(s): _____
Guest of: (i.e., you, your daughter and her fiancé, or his parents)

_____

Attending: Yes ❑ No ❑

Name of guest(s): _____
Guest of: (i.e., you, your daughter and her fiancé, or his parents)

_____

Attending: Yes ❑ No ❑

Name of guest(s): _____
Guest of: (i.e., you, your daughter and her fiancé, or his parents)

_____

Attending: Yes ❑ No ❑

Name of guest(s): _____
Guest of: (i.e., you, your daughter and her fiancé, or his parents)

_____

Attending: Yes ❑ No ❑

Name of guest(s): _____
Guest of: (i.e., you, your daughter and her fiancé, or his parents)

_____

Attending: Yes ❑ No ❑

Name of guest(s): _____
Guest of: (i.e., you, your daughter and her fiancé,
or his parents)

_____

Attending: Yes ❑ No ❑

Name of guest(s): _____
Guest of: (i.e., you, your daughter and her fiancé,
or his parents)

_____

Attending: Yes ❑ No ❑

Name of guest(s): _____
Guest of: (i.e., you, your daughter and her fiancé,
or his parents)

_____

Attending: Yes ❑ No ❑

Name of guest(s): _____
Guest of: (i.e., you, your daughter and her fiancé,
or his parents)

_____

Attending: Yes ❑ No ❑

Name of guest(s): _____
Guest of: (i.e., you, your daughter and her fiancé,
or his parents)

_____

Attending: Yes ❑ No ❑

Name of guest(s): _____
Guest of: (i.e., you, your daughter and her fiancé,
or his parents)

_____

Attending: Yes ❑ No ❑

Dress Information

For your daughter:

Color: _____

Designer: _____

Style number: _____

Size: _____

Price: _____

Alteration fees: _____

Date for fitting: _____

Date alterations are due: _____

Date for second fitting: _____

Date alterations are due: _____

For you:

Color: _____

Designer: _____

Style number: _____

Size: _____

Price: _____

Alteration fees: _____

Date for fitting: _____

Date alterations are due: _____

Date for second fitting: _____

Date alterations are due: _____

Wedding-Day Checklists

For your daughter:

Does she have …

- ❏ Hosiery (2 pair)
- ❏ Proper undergarments
- ❏ Shoes
- ❏ Gloves
- ❏ Veil
- ❏ Slip/crinoline
- ❏ Dress
- ❏ Jewelry
- ❏ Something old
- ❏ Something new
- ❏ Something borrowed
- ❏ Something blue
- ❏ Makeup
- ❏ Purse
- ❏ Penoit/lingerie for wedding night

For you:

- ❏ Hosiery (2 pair)
- ❏ Proper undergarments
- ❏ Shoes
- ❏ Gloves
- ❏ Hat
- ❏ Dress/suit

- ❏ Jewelry
- ❏ Makeup for wedding day
- ❏ Purse
- ❏ Sewing kit
- ❏ Phone numbers of all wedding-day vendors
- ❏ Safety pins
- ❏ Clear nail polish (for hosiery runs)

Resources

Websites

All-Encompassing Wedding Sites

www.ultimatewedding.com

Although there are lots of ads to wade through (not uncommon for wedding sites in general), this site offers multiple online wedding-planning tools, including a vendor organizer, bride's journal (hey, there's nothing saying it can't be a mother-of-the-bride journal!), and personal calendar. There's also lots of wedding-planning advice; although it's all couched in an article format, much of it is from their community message board. Sometimes, though, the latter deals with more pertinent information.

www.ourmarriage.com

A great, easily navigable site that deals with a plethora of practical advice, from the basic (bride's emergency wedding-day checklist) to modern wedding conundrums and questions (what *does* the mother of the groom do, exactly?). There's also a nice section on ethnic and cultural traditions from around the world. Also, check out the Local Wedding Vendors section, where you can click on your state and look for potential photographers, wedding planners, DJs, etc.

www.weddinginsight.com

Not as sleek and slightly hokier looking than sites like The Knot, but a good source for basic wedding information and tips.

www.weddingchannel.com

Fantastic site that actually has a section called "Wedding Party and Family" that speaks directly to the mother of the bride, mother of the groom, attendants, etc. (this, you will soon find out, is rare). Be sure to check out the article on how one mother of the bride and mother of the groom learned to work together, and even eventually became friends. Links you to major department store registries as well.

www.theknot.com

The site that took weddings and wedding planning to a whole new level of sophistication. The Knot combines modern sensibilities and issues with tradition and custom. The Knot shop is overpriced and we advise that you shop around before purchasing anything from their store, but don't miss the very informative Ask Carley section and interactive wedding-planning tools.

www.weddingzone.net

Aesthetically it's a bit of a cheese ball that's big on ads and low on content, but the local vendor sources are very helpful.

Gown Preservation

www.heritagegown.com

After your daughter and son-in-law skip off to their honeymoon, it's entirely likely that you'll be holding on to the wedding dress. You might even be given the task of sending it to the cleaners or to find a place to preserve it if your daughter plans to hold on to it. If you don't have a reputable source nearby, Heritage Gown, which is based in California, provides free shipping and museum-quality preservation techniques. They also offer a do-it-yourself preservation kit for about ninety bucks if you're a hands-on kind of gal.

Dresses

www.davidsbridal.com

Extremely affordable wedding dresses, bridesmaid attire, and—eureka!—outfits for the mom of the bride, too. Good sales make the prices even better than they already are. Watch out for the alteration costs, though—they sometimes are even more than the dress.

www.bargainweddinggowns.com

It looks a little like a Sunday circular online, but the prices are good and there's a mom-of-the-bride section as well that even offers plus sizes.

www.elegantgowns.com

Name-brand wedding dresses, etc., discounted 20 to 40 percent off the regular retail price. Particularly handy if you've been out shopping and your daughter sees a dress that she likes but is out of your price range. Write down the make and style number, type it into the box provided on the elegantgowns site, and there's a good chance you'll find it. Wedding tips, calendars, and other interactive tools, too.

www.bluefly.com

No wedding dresses, but lots of great, heavily discounted brand-name dresses for you and, potentially, the wedding party. Shoes, jewelry, and handbags, too.

Transportation

www.limo.org

The official website of the National Limousine Association. Allows you to find a reputable vendor near you.

Books

Aloni, Nicole. *Secrets from a Caterer's Kitchen.* New York: HP Books, 2001.

If you can't hire a pro, why not get advice from one? From party-planning strategy to great recipes, this book is a solid resource for anyone who's looking for hostess-with-the-mostest status.

Cowie, Colin. *Weddings*. New York: Little Brown Publishers, 1998.

Cowie's got more style and pizzazz in his little pinky than most of us can muster in a lifetime. Chock-full of great ideas, this book is pricey but if you're the planner in charge, Cowie's expertise is a good thing to have in your corner. From city to country to southern, this book offers several different types of wedding samples.

Garten, Ina. *The Barefoot Contessa Parties! Ideas and Recipes for Easy Parties That Are Really Fun*. New York: Clarkson Potter, 2001.

A former White House budget analyst, Ina Garten traded her conservative suits for simple white aprons back in 1978 and she's had us salivating ever since. This book (and, really, any of her books) gives delicious, *easy* (really!), recipes for great party snacks and meals that will impress without stress. You will use this book again and again.

Lata Rung, Jennifer. *The Pocket Idiot's Guide to Being the Father of the Bride*. Indianapolis: Alpha Books, 2003.

If your daughter's dad is feeling a little left out of the loop, hand him a copy of this great little pocket guide to get him up to speed on his daughter's big day.

Lendermen, Teddy. *The Complete Idiot's Guide to the Perfect Wedding*, 3rd Edition. Indianapolis: Alpha Books, 2000.

The wonderful, creative, and clever Teddy Lendermen leads you through wedding planning from start to finish.

Post, Peggy. *Emily Post's Wedding Etiquette: Cherished Traditions and Contemporary Ideas for a Joyous Celebration*, 4th Edition. New York: HarperCollins, 2001.

Post is the oracle of weddings. A must for any bride or mother of.

Sachs, Patty, and Phyllis Cambria. *The Complete Idiot's Guide to Throwing a Great Party*. Indianapolis: Alpha Books, 2000.

Party Planning 101 from ladies who know!

Stewart, Martha. *The Best of Martha Stewart Weddings*. New York: Clarkson Potter, 1999.

Behind bars or not, Stewart still reigns supreme as the elegant do-it-yourself maven. This book offers lots and lots to create a gorgeous wedding day for your daughter, from ceremony to reception.

Vandermeer, Anthonia. *The Complete Idiot's Guide to Creative Weddings*. Indianapolis: Alpha Books, 1999.

From the beach to the barn, Vandermeer gives great ideas on how to add serious pizzazz and personality to any wedding.

Handy-Dandy Glossary

Of course, you've been through this already and know the ins and outs, but just in case some of the lingo escapes you, we've compiled a list of helpful terms that will be here for you if you need it.

A-line   Cut of a dress that's narrow at the waist but flows out in an A shape from the bodice. The most flattering cut for any body.

Aroosi   The post-nuptial Iranian celebratory party marked by a lavish meal of whole roasted lamb and two kinds of rice, Morrasah Polo ("jeweled" rice) Shirin Polo (sweet rice).

bandeau   A bodice style for a dress characterized by its straight, tight-fitting, band-shaped nature.

barong tagalog   An almost translucent ecru-colored linen shirt with ornate embroidery on the front. Worn untucked by a Filipino groom, with a white T-shirt underneath and black pants.

bateau   Also referred to as a boat neckline, this is characterized by its straight-across shape from shoulder to shoulder.

birkat hamazon   An after-meal grace said after the *seudah mitzfah* at a Jewish wedding.

bone china   Translucent, thin, white or creamy fine China that uses bone ash as an ingredient.

boutonniere   A small, demure flower arrangement or single flower worn by men on the lapel of their jacket.

Brahmin   A Hindu priest.

brundlaupskling   The Swedish wedding feast generally dominated by a buffet of Swedish foods. In particular, a Swedish sweet bread is often featured.

buffet   A dinner style where the food is presented on tables where guests serve themselves.

carre   In a French ceremony, the silk canopy where nuptials occur that is supposed to protect the bride and groom from bad luck.

cathedral length   The longest train a wedding dress may have (think Princess Diana).

chapel length   A train that extends several feet behind a wedding dress.

charmeuse   Lightweight, soft satin fabric.

chiffon   Lightweight, sheer material with a lustrous, almost opalescent sheen.

chupah   A canopy beneath which Jewish nuptials are held.

Claddagh ring   A ring in the shape of two hands (representing faith) that hold a heart (representing love) that wears a crown (representing honor). Is sometimes used as a wedding ring by Irish couples.

coupe de mariage   In France, a two-handled engraved goblet the bride and groom drink from during the first toast.

corsage   A small, demure flower arrangement worn by the mother of the bride and mother of the groom. It is either pinned to the woman's attire or worn on the wrist.

chiffon   Lightweight, lustrous, sheer, and often layered fabric.

chiverie   After a French wedding, the act of guests showing up at the bride and groom's home (or room, if in a hotel or inn), banging pots and singing songs until the couple invites them in for a drink and something to eat.

croquembouche   In France, a special "cake" served at a wedding, made of small pastry puffs filled with cream, covered with glaze, and shaped like a pyramid.

crystal   High-quality, beautiful glassware often with decorative cuts and designs. Contains a per-centage of lead in the glass and is very fragile.

cummerbund   A thick sash worn around a man's waist and over the top of his pants, usually with a tuxedo.

earthenware   Dishes, cups, etc., made from clay.

"Eviva gli sposi!"   An Italian wedding toast that means "Hurray for the newlyweds!"

Fattah   The traditional food of an Egyptian ceremony, which consists of lamb in rice and bread dipped in a stew.

fiancé   Man engaged to be married.

fiancée   Woman engaged to be married.

flatware   Forks, knives, spoons, serving pieces, and other dining and serving utensils.

goshugi   In Japan, a wedding gift of money in a decorative envelope.

hochzeitssuppe   A traditional German wedding soup made of beef, dumplings, and vegetables.

hora   A dance at a Jewish wedding performed by the newly married couple and their guests. The couple are each seated in a chair and hold a handkerchief between them. They are hoisted into the air by male guests, while the rest of the celebrants join hands and dance in a circle around them.

kalamatiano   In Greece, the traditional dance performed by the bride and groom, during which the bride and groom dance together while each hold an end of the same scarf.

kolache   A traditional Czech wedding pastry usually made with fruit.

kosha   In Egyptian receptions, two special seats reserved for the new couple where guests can greet them and they can act as "king and queen" of the festivities.

koufeta   White-coated almonds given to wedding guests in Greece as a symbol of the simultaneous sweetness and bitterness of life. An odd number should be counted for each gift to represent good luck.

ketubah   In the Jewish faith, a marriage contract signed by the couple beforehand and read aloud during the ceremony. It is given to the bride and groom after the ceremony ends.

krenzl   If it is your only or last daughter who is being married, it is traditional at a Jewish wedding to perform a *krenzl*—seat the mother of the bride in the center of the room and have her daughter or daughters crown her with flowers and dance around her chair.

lazo   In Mexican weddings, a long rosary that is draped over both the bride and groom at the altar to represent their joining together.

Maid of Honor   Unmarried woman, chosen by the bride, who is responsible for standing up for and next to the bride during the ceremony. She acts as an official witness for the marriage certificate, and throws the bridal shower.

Matron of Honor Married woman chosen by the bride who performs the same duties as the maid of honor.

mead A type of wine made from honey, water, and yeast, consumed by the bride and groom and guests at an Irish wedding.

menyasszonytanc A traditional Hungarian wedding dance during which guests pay to dance with the bride—and the price goes up with each dance!

monogram The couple's initials engraved or embroidered onto various items (silver, linens, robes, etc.).

nazmenet In Hungary, a bridal procession, led by an uncle of the bride, to the reception.

nosegay A small, round arrangement or bouquet of flowers.

oczepiny A ceremony performed at a Polish reception, where the bride's veil is removed to represent her movement from a maid to a married woman.

officiant Person who performs a wedding ceremony.

organza Chiffon-like fabric, only heavier and stiffer.

Paella Valenciana A popular main course at a Spanish wedding, made of saffron rice with chicken, sausages, and seafood.

palinka A drink offered to guests as they arrive at a Hungarian reception. It is a strong brandy usually consumed as a shot.

Pandango   A special dance performed by the Filipino bride and groom, where guests pin money to the couple to help pay for their honeymoon.

penoir   Often elegant, but definitely sexy matching robe and nightgown set often worn on the wedding night by the bride.

peplum   Either attached to the bodice or skirt, this is a decorative swathe of material surrounding the hips.

polteraband   In the traditional three-day German celebration, the name of the celebratory reception held on the second day.

porcelain   Similar to bone china, but not as fine or translucent.

receiving line   The face-out line formed by the bride, groom, and their parents to greet and receive congratulations from their guests after the ceremony.

sangria   A wine punch made with fresh fruit served at a traditional Mexican wedding reception.

sequidilla manchega   A dance performed at a Spanish wedding, where guests dance with the bride and give her money.

seudah mitzfah   A celebratory meal eaten at a Jewish wedding reception.

shantung   Silk fabric with a nubby texture.

silverplate   Flatware that is coated with pure silver, but is not made entirely of silver.

skullcap   Also called a yarmulke, this is a small, round cap worn by Jewish males during religious ceremonies and meetings.

smorgasbord   A Swedish buffet dinner.

stainless steel   Flatware made of an alloy steel, chromium. It's rust resistant and dishwasher safe, unlike sterling or silverplated flatware.

sterling   Flatware made of solid sterling silver.

stoneware   Dinnerware that's made of clay and generally rustic in look. Good for everyday dishes.

taffeta   Stiff fabric that can be matte or shiny, often used for bride's or bridesmaid's gowns.

tarantella   A traditional Italian dance often performed by guests at the reception.

trousseau   The entire makeup of the bride's wedding wardrobe. Consists of wedding gown; lingerie; accessories; honeymoon wardrobe; and new household linens.

tulle   Netlike, mesh material that's often used underneath the skirt of wedding or bridesmaid's gowns to give it some "poof." Can be used over material as well.

unity candle   One usually fairly large white candle that is lit by the bride and groom to represent their new life together.

yihun   After the nuptials in a Jewish wedding and prior to the ceremony, a ritual where the bride and groom may go off to another room alone. Here they will sit alone and eat a simple soup together. The word translates to mean "union."

zaffa   In an Egyptian wedding, this is a processional with rousing music and belly dancers, flaming swordsman, and drummers and horns that occurs before the exchange of vows.

Index

84025